EUREKA!

The Life and Times
of Archimedes

EUREKA!

[EYPEKA!]

The Life and Times of Archimedes

A musical play in one act

by John Trevillion

Music by Jeff Spade

Book, lyrics, and additional music by John Trevillion

Waldorf
PUBLICATIONS
RESEARCH INSTITUTE FOR Waldorf EDUCATION

Printed with support from the Waldorf Curriculum Fund

Published by:

Waldorf Publications at the
Research Institute for Waldorf Education
38 Main Street
Chatham, NY 12037

Title: *Eureka! The Life and Times of Archimedes*
A play in one act by John Trevillion
Music by Jeffrey Spade and John Trevillion
Lyrics by John Trevillion

Cover: Leah McDowell
Proofreader: Colleen Shetland
Layout: Ann Erwin

© 2016 Waldorf Publications
ISBN # 978-1-936367-88-7

CAST OF CHARACTERS

Archimedes:	inventor, scientist, geometer
Hieron:	king of Syracuse, Archimedes' brother-in-law
Helena:	Archimedes' wife
Marcus Claudius Marcellus:	leader of Roman army besieging Syracuse
Lucius:	Archimedes' slave, son of Tiberius
Livia:	Archimedes' slave, daughter of Tiberius
Epikydes:	tyrant of Syracuse, seized by force
Hieronymus:	Hieron's grandson
Eratosthenes:	Archimedes' son
Phidias:	Archimedes' father
Arête:	Archimedes' mother
Tiberius:	Archimedes' slave
Cornelia:	Archimedes' slave, wife to Tiberius
Straton:	Syracusan officer
Phineas:	a goldsmith
Philistis:	Hieron's wife
Leptines:	Hieron's first minister
Gelon:	Hieron's son
Adranodorus:	Hieron's son-in-law
Damarata:	Hieron's daughter
Quinctius Crispinus:	Roman officer
Appius Claudius Pulcher:	Roman officer
Gaius Septimus:	Roman legionary
Marcus:	Roman legionary
Braxus:	Roman legionary
Crassus:	Roman legionary
Servant to Hieron	
Servant to Hieron	

SETTING

Scenes 1–3 occur during the final stages of the siege of Syracuse by the Roman army during the Second Punic War in 211 BC, both within the Roman camp and inside the walls of Greek Syracuse. Through the characters of LUCIUS and LIVIA, household slaves of ARCHIMEDES, they provide the sympathetic General MARCELLUS with glimpses into the life of ARCHIMEDES, the domestic tension with his fiery wife, HELENA, and his friendly relation to HIERON, king of Syracuse, who by some accounts was brother-in-law to ARCHIMEDES.

Scenes 4–8 capture these moments some 40 years earlier when Syracuse enjoyed peace and prosperity. These scenes alternate between ARCHIMEDES' courtyard and the palace court of Hieron.

Scenes 9–12 return to the time-frame of the siege and illustrate the circumstances which drew Rome into conflict with Syracuse, and the final assault on Syracuse, the attempted but failed rescue of ARCHIMEDES and his family. (Note: Actors could assume multiple parts other than those of ARCHIMEDES, HIERON, HELENA, and MARCELLUS.)

SCENE 1

SETTING: (Marcus Claudius MARCELLUS, the commanding general of the
             Roman army, which has been engaged in a three-year long siege of
             Syracuse, a Greek city-state on the island of Sicily, meets in council
             with his subordinate commanding officers, L. Quinctius CRISPINUS,
             commander of the navy, and Appius CLAUDIUS Pulcher, commanding
             officer of the land army)

MARCELLUS
These Greeks are laughing at us. Three years we have besieged their city, and they
are no closer to surrender than they were when we began, Quinctius.

CRISPINUS
Sir.

MARCELLUS
I stood on the heights above the city this morning and saw boats – Greek boats,
Egyptian boats, *Carthaginian boats*, for Jupiter's sake – sailing in and out as if it were
peacetime! These Greeks are better fed than our own troops! Why can't you stop this
traffic?

CRISPINUS
General Marcellus, with all due respect, you know as well as I do. The entrance to the
two harbors is too wide to choke off. If we could get in close enough to the city, we
might be able to close off traffic, but we've tried that…many times.

MARCELLUS
Then you must try again.

CRISPINUS
You know what would happen. The enemy would open fire on us again, and re-
ignite the terror in our sailors. They already have! Even last week a convoy of our
ships patrolled the coast at what we thought was a more than a safe distance when,
whoosh, out of nowhere a rock of immense size hurtled in and sank one of the ships.
Grown men – seasoned soldiers! – cowered on the decks like frightened children. I
have given orders to patrol even further from the walls of Syracuse.

             *(MARCELLUS looks at him disapprovingly;
             CRISPINUS gestures in frustration)*

I *had* to give the order! The men would refuse to sail if I didn't. *(pause)* But why bother? What good do our patrols do?

MARCELLUS

> *(looks at CRISPINUS a moment longer as if about to reprimand him, changes his mind, and turns to the other officer present)*

Claudius, how is the morale among the land troops?

CLAUDIUS

Bored, weary, anxious to go home, Sir. They have not seen their families in three years. They worry that their wives and children are starving to death. Who will till their lands? How will the taxes be paid? Who can blame them for such thoughts?

MARCELLUS

Claudius, *I* would like to go home to my wife and children, but I have a job to do. So do you...and we haven't yet done it!

CLAUDIUS

I understand, Sir, but these men came to fight, not to sit and wait like this. They long for action, blood, and plunder. I...

MARCELLUS

Yes?

CLAUDIUS

I hear whispers of mutiny, Sir.

MARCELLUS

How far do think it has gone?

CLAUDIUS

Not far...yet. But if this waiting should go on much longer...

MARCELLUS

Have we discovered any weak points along the enemy walls yet?

CLAUDIUS

We can't get close enough to find out. Every time we send scouts to reconnoiter...

MARCELLUS

I know, I know! Archimedes' weapons drive them back. What I would give to have that man on our side!

(a long pause as the men look at each other waiting for one of them to speak. They have clearly had this conversation many times before, and frustration is in evidence)

CRISPINUS
General Marcellus, we are at war with Carthage. It is *Carthage* that wishes to destroy Rome, not these Syracusans. Couldn't we just…

MARCELLUS
Retreat? Out of the question. Syracuse has pledged allegiance to Carthage, and a friend of Rome's enemy is an enemy of Rome. It's as simple as that.

CLAUDIUS
But Syracuse has no interest in destroying Rome. For the last fifty years she has been Rome's steadfast ally…

MARCELLUS
It wouldn't matter if it had been a thousand years of friendship. Once Epikydes allied Syracuse to Carthage, he sealed his city's doom.

CRISPINUS
But…

MARCELLUS
Enough! This is idle chatter. The Senate would laugh at such talk. No, much worse! They would have us put to death for treason! Pull yourselves together! We are Romans!

(to a march rhythm. CRISPINUS and CLAUDIUS [and possibly a larger chorus] provide the "We Are Romans")

A ROMAN DOES NOT PANIC IN THE FRAY,
(WE ARE ROMANS, WE ARE ROMANS)
NO MATTER WHAT THE ODDS HE WILL OBEY,
(WE ARE ROMANS, WE ARE ROMANS)

HE'LL SACRIFICE HIS LIFE TO SAVE THE CITY OF HIS BIRTH,
HE'LL FIGHT TO SAVE HER HONOR WITH EV'RYTHING HE'S WORTH,
HE'S LOYAL TO THE CITY THAT WILL ONE DAY RULE THE EARTH:
THIS NOBLE CAUSE HE NEVER WOULD BETRAY.

A ROMAN MARCHES TO A SINGLE BEAT,
(WE ARE ROMANS, WE ARE ROMANS)
HE DOESN'T KNOW THE MEANING OF RETREAT,
(WE ARE ROMANS, WE ARE ROMANS)

HE'LL SACRIFICE HIS LIFE TO SAVE THE CITY OF HIS BIRTH,
HE'LL FIGHT TO SAVE HER HONOR WITH EV'RYTHING HE'S WORTH,
HE'S LOYAL TO THE CITY THAT WILL ONE DAY RULE THE EARTH:
ALL ENEMIES OF ROME HE WILL DEFEAT.

A ROMAN NEVER CALCULATES THE COST,
(WE ARE ROMANS, WE ARE ROMANS)
HE NEVER WILL ADMIT THE BATTLE'S LOST,
(WE ARE ROMANS, WE ARE ROMANS)

HE'LL SACRIFICE HIS LIFE TO SAVE THE CITY OF HIS BIRTH,
HE'LL FIGHT TO SAVE HER HONOR WITH EV'RYTHING HE'S WORTH,
HE'S LOYAL TO THE CITY THAT WILL ONE DAY RULE THE EARTH:
TO SERVE HER EV'RY MEASURE HE'LL EXHAUST.

WE ARE ROMANS, WE ARE ROMANS
WE ARE ROMANS, WE ARE ROMANS
WE ARE ROMANS, WE ARE ROMANS
WE ARE ROMANS, WE ARE ROMANS
WE ARE ROMANS, WE ARE ROMANS
WE ARE ROMANS, WE ARE ROMANS

HE'LL SACRIFICE HIS LIFE TO SAVE THE CITY OF HIS BIRTH,
HE'LL FIGHT TO SAVE HER HONOR WITH EVERYTHING HE'S WORTH,
HE'S LOYAL TO THE CITY THAT WILL ONE DAY RULE THE EARTH:
TO SERVE HER EV'RY MEASURE HE'LL EXHAUST.

WE ARE ROMANS, WE ARE ROMANS, etc.

MARCELLUS
There must be some way to get close to those walls.

CLAUDIUS
Well, we have agreed with Epikydes to an exchange of prisoners tomorrow at the gate of Galeagra.

MARCELLUS
At the gate...yes, we'll never have a better opportunity! Claudius, when we meet with the Greek officers at the gate, I want you to estimate the height of walls, but don't make it obvious what you are doing. At least we will know the height of those walls and can build ladders of sufficient height to scale them.

CLAUDIUS
A clever plan, Sir, but once we have built those ladders, how will we get close enough to those walls to use them?

MARCELLUS
One step at a time, Claudius. One step at a time.

SCENE 2

SETTING: (EPIKYDES, tyrant of Syracuse, stands above the gate of Galeagra with STRATON, a senior officer of the Syracusan army, looking down on the scene [which can be imaginary] of the prisoner exchange)

EPIKYDES
(without sympathy)
By the looks of it the Romans have not treated our men very kindly. They look miserable!

STRATON
They will need much rest and food before they are ready to fight for us again, Excellency.

EPIKYDES
Well, it's their good fortune to be coming home for the Feast of Artemis, isn't it? Or is it Diana now? Oh well, never mind. A good excuse for a celebration either way.

STRATON
Food is scarce, my lord.

EPIKYDES
But not drink. They will forget their sorrows soon enough.

STRATON
No doubt, Excellency, though I warrant most of them will have little heart for the occasion.

EPIKYDES
Eh?

STRATON
Most of them are mercenaries. Lord. They worship foreign gods.

EPIKYDES
(disinterested, looking down immediately below)
Yes, well…Ah, here come *our* prisoners. Hmm, they don't look so well either.

STRATON
(chuckling)
A few months working in our stone quarries will do that to a person.

EPIKYDES
Indeed it will. Why are *those* prisoners not wearing Roman uniforms? Wait! Isn't that one a woman? Hard to tell beneath all that dirt.

STRATON
Those are suspected Roman sympathizers, my Lord. You ordered them to be part of the exchange, you remember?

EPIKYDES
Yes, of course, I remember. Good riddance.
(pause – again, pointing)
Look at how close those Roman soldiers are! Which one is Marcellus?

STRATON
Over there, my Lord.

EPIKYDES
Yes, I recognize him now. I fought against him.

STRATON
My Lord?

EPIKYDES
When I marched with Hannibal's army. Three times we tried to take the city of Nola from the Romans, and three times we were repulsed. It was Hannibal's first taste of real resistance from these Romans. Marcellus was their commander.

STRATON
And now he threatens Syracuse.

EPIKYDES
You sound worried.

STRATON
Well, it was Hannibal after all.

EPIKYDES
Hannibal didn't have our weapons, Straton.
                (His gaze lingers on MARCELLUS.)
He looks *very* serious, doesn't he? Hmph! I have to hand it to these Romans. They are tenacious! Greeks would have called off such a futile siege two years ago. Carthaginians would not have even bothered to *begin* such a siege! Couldn't we simply load one of Archimedes' catapults right now and rid ourselves of this tiresome Roman?

STRATON
But...what about our own officers, my Lord, and the prisoners? Wouldn't they be killed, too?

EPIKYDES
Yes? And...?
                (STRATON is lost for words.)
Speaking of Archimedes, what is that old scribbler up to, anyway?

STRATON
He inspects the weaponry every morning, but otherwise he stays at home.

EPIKYDES
Doing what?

STRATON
Doing what...what he does when he's by himself, I suppose. I don't know what he does.

EPIKYDES
His precious geometry! He deigns to look at his weapons when *he* feels like it, then goes off to make drawings in the sand. Never mind that there's a war going on! I've a mind to send him to the quarries to gather his own ammunition.

STRATON
Then who would...?

EPIKYDES
Protect Syracuse? Calm yourself, Straton, I would not be so foolish as to rid Syracuse of its protector. Still, the man is lucky it is I who rule Syracuse.

STRATON
(with just a hint of irony)
Lucky indeed, my Lord.

EPIKYDES
Well, this *has* been most pleasant, but I suppose I must attend Marcellus and make this exchange official. Then there are the festival preparations. Pity you won't be able to join the festivities, Straton. Keep a sober eye on these Romans, eh?

(STRATON bows as EPIKYDES exits.)

SCENE 3

SETTING: (The Roman camp, where MARCELLUS holds council once more
             with CLAUDIUS)

MARCELLUS
And you counted the rows of stones successfully?

CLAUDIUS
I did, Sir.

MARCELLUS
And you are confident of your estimate?

CLAUDIUS
I am, Sir. Those walls are massive! These Greeks, they build...well, they build almost as well as we Romans, Sir.

MARCELLUS
What about the ladders?

CLAUDIUS
I have crews working on them as we speak, Sir.

MARCELLUS
Good. Now to get close enough to use them.

CLAUDIUS
(brightening)
During the prisoner exchange a few of them were overheard speaking of a celebration to take place in two days' time. The Festival of Artemis, they called it.

MARCELLUS
Artemis?

CLAUDIUS
Aye, Sir, our Diana...though the Greeks claim Artemis came first.

MARCELLUS
(indifferent)
Do they? How long will this festival last?

CLAUDIUS
A week. There will be much feasting and drinking, they said. Mostly drinking, actually. Food is scarce. And *everyone* is expected to participate.

MARCELLUS
Everyone?

CLAUDIUS
Aye, Sir, there's every likelihood the sentries on the wall will enjoy their share of the fun, too. And why wouldn't they? It's been three years for them.

MARCELLUS
So you think we should give them a few days to get plastered, and then...

CLAUDIUS
...we go in by night. It just might work, Sir.

MARCELLUS
No, Claudius, it *must* work. This is our opportunity and we must seize it.

CLAUDIUS
Perhaps the gods are smiling on us at last.

MARCELLUS
The gods? I do not know whether the gods smile or frown. I don't even know if they care. But I do know that if we do not take this opportunity now, we are lost.

(A soldier approaches. He salutes MARCELLUS and CLAUDIUS, stands at attention, looking away into the distance. Behind him stand two disheveled and dirty prisoners. One is a man and the other a woman. They look down at the ground.)

GAIUS
Sir!

MARCELLUS
Name?

GAIUS
Gaius Septimus, sir. Second Legion.

MARCELLUS
At ease, soldier. What is it?

GAIUS
Sir, these slaves were among the prisoner exchange today, Sir.

MARCELLUS
And?

GAIUS
Sir, they claim to be of Roman descent, Sir.

MARCELLUS
Yes, well we knew there would be Roman sympathizers in the exchange. Unless there is something else, soldier, we have business here...

GAIUS
Sir, they were slaves belonging to that Greek fellow, Archimedes. Isn't that what he's called, the one who bedevils us with his catapults and such?

MARCELLUS
(suddenly very interested)
Bring them forward.

GAIUS
Aye, Sir.

(He escorts the two slaves forward, then stands aside. The slaves look down.)

MARCELLUS
Who are you? Tell me your names.

LUCIUS
My name, sir, is Lucius, and this is my sister, Livia. At least, that's what Master called us.

MARCELLUS
And who was your master?

LUCIUS
Archimedes.

MARCELLUS
The inventor?

LUCIUS
Aye, sir, the same.

MARCELLUS
You speak Latin well. Hardly a trace of accent.

LUCIUS
Our parents were Romans, sir. They were captured by the Carthaginians in the first war with Carthage and sold into slavery.

MARCELLUS
Your hard luck. I'm sorry.

LIVIA
Oh no, sir, it wasn't hard luck at all.

MARCELLUS
(a little surprised a woman is speaking)
Being sold into slavery is not hard luck? What do you mean?

LIVIA
Well, sir, it was and it wasn't, if you see what I mean.

MARCELLUS
What *do* you mean?

LIVIA
Well, sir, our parents were bought by Phidias – that's Archimedes' father – to serve his children. And there aren't kinder souls on earth than Phidias, his wife, and his children.

MARCELLUS
They've treated you well?

LIVIA
As members of the family, sir.

MARCELLUS
So...how long have you served Archimedes?

LUCIUS
I served Archimedes, sir. My sister, she served Helena.

MARCELLUS
And who is Helena?

LUCIUS
Archimedes' wife.

MARCELLUS
How long have you served Archimedes?

LUCIUS
Since I was very young, sir. Not long after Archimedes had returned.

MARCELLUS
Returned? From where?

LUCIUS
From Alexandria, sir. He'd been gone, they told me, for several years. To study - you know, geometry and such things as only master understands well.

LIVIA
At the Museum. That's what he called the place he worked at.

MARCELLUS
(now profoundly interested)
> *(He summons CLAUDIUS to the other side of the tent out of earshot of the slaves.)*

Claudius, go prepare the men for the assault. Tell them the long wait is over. And be sure those ladders are ready.

CLAUDIUS
It will be a pleasure, sir.

MARCELLUS
(to GAIUS)
Soldier, stand guard outside.

GAIUS
Aye, Sir.
>   *(exit)*

MARCELLUS
(to LUCIUS and LIVIA)
Sit down.
>   *(They squat.)*

No, on the chairs. Now tell me all about your master, Archimedes. Spare me no detail. I want to know all about him.

LUCIUS
(looking with some surprise and bewilderment at his sister)
Aye, sir. Where would you like me to begin?

MARCELLUS
At the beginning, when you first met him.

LUCIUS
Well, we were very young, you know, but there are some things I'll never forget.

MARCELLUS
Go on.

SCENE 4

SETTING: (In the inner courtyard of PHIDIAS' home in Syracuse. PHIDIAS, very old, lies on a couch, watching his grandchild play. He occasionally smiles and chuckles in delight. ARÊTE, his wife, sits next to HELENA, ARCHIMEDES' wife.)

They are weaving. Occupied with work by himself is TIBERIUS, servant to PHIDIAS and ARCHIMEDES. Near him stands CORNELIA, his wife, and servant to ARÊTE and HELENA, preparing food for dinner. She keeps a watchful eye on her children, young LUCIUS and LIVIA. LUCIUS and LIVIA are playing a game of catch with ARCHIMEDES' son, ERATOSTHENES. They use a cloth ball. ARCHIMEDES sits visibly on the second floor of the house where he is engaged in a geometric problem. He holds a large wooden compass in his hand and can be seen occasionally using it to trace patterns on his sand-board. He is utterly absorbed in his problem, and pays no attention to the activities below him.

ERATOSTHENES
Let's see how high we can throw it.

(*LUCIUS and LIVIA giggle at the fun and the game proceeds with the ball going ever higher.*)

ARÊTE
Now, children, be careful where you throw it.

ERATOSTHENES
We will.

CORNELIA
And that goes for you, too, Lucius and Livia. Don't disturb Master, do you hear?

LUCIUS AND LIVIA
(*like ERATOSTHENES, absorbed in the game*)
We won't, Mama. Higher!

HELENA
Are you alright, Papa? I hope you are not too hot in the sun.
Should we move you into the shade?

PHIDIAS
No, thank you, dear, I'm fine. I'm enjoying myself almost as much as the children.

ERATOSTHENES
Alright, Papa, but you tell me if you get too hot.

PHIDIAS
I will.

HELENA
Medion? Are you thirsty? Aren't you hot up there?

> *(ARCHIMEDES seems not to hear her and merely inscribes another circle. HELENA looks at the other women with a familiar, knowing shrug.)*

Is he hot? Is he thirsty? He's too absorbed in his work to even know if he's hungry or thirsty.
> *(She crosses to CORNELIA.)*
Cornelia, when will the evening meal be ready?

CORNELIA
Very soon, mistress. Maybe another half hour.

HELENA
(tasting the soup)
More salt.

CORNELIA
Yes, mistress.

HELENA
Medion, don't forget, King Hicron wants to see you tomorrow. When was the last time you bathed?
> *(no reply)*
You have to take a bath, okay? And wear a clean chiton!
> *(again, no reply)*
Dinner will be ready soon!
> *(to ARETÊ)*
I might as well be speaking to the wall. If it weren't for me, that man would *never* eat or drink. I have an easier time getting the children's attention than his. Ugh! He's impossible!

ARÊTE
(patting her daughter-in-law's hand)
He can't help it, dear. It's just who he is. He was just as remote when he was a little boy.

HELENA
How did you ever manage? I mean, not to lose your temper with him?

ARÊTE
Oh, I *did* lose my temper...at first.
(her hand shielding her mouth from PHIDIAS)
But you know, he's no different from his father. They are both cut from the same strange cloth. If I spent my days being upset with them, I'd have been old when I was your age.

ERATOSTHENES
(to his playmates)
Watch this.

> *(He throws the ball with both hands as high as he can. It lands in ARCHIMEDES' sand-board.)*

ARCHIMEDES
Eh? What's this? How did...?

> *(He realizes suddenly how the ball arrived to interrupt his contemplation. He picks up the ball and stands at the edge of the platform, looking down at the children below. They are very silent and a little afraid, knowing that ARCHIMEDES should never be interrupted in his work. ERATOSTHENES hides behind LUCIUS.)*

Alright, which one of you children threw this?
> *(no answer)*
I said, which one of you children threw this?

ERATOSTHENES
I did, Papa.

ARCHIMEDES
How many times have I told you not to interrupt me when I'm busy?

ERATOSTHENES
I didn't mean to throw it on the roof, Papa, really I didn't.

ARCHIMEDES
Well, you've landed your ball right in the middle of my drawing. Worse! You've landed it right in the middle of my thought!

HELENA
> *(striding over and putting her arms around*
> *ERATOSTHENES, then looking up at her husband sharply)*
Medion! What does Eratosthenes know about interrupting thoughts? He's just a boy!

ARCHIMEDES
Yes, but…I was *this close* to the solution, and now it's gone!

HELENA
(to ERATOSTHENES)
You see that pot over there? Why don't you and Lucius and Livia have a contest to see who can throw it into the pot first?

ERATOSTHENES
> *(brightening at the possibility)*
Okay, Mama!
> *(looking at his playmates)*
I get first shot.

HELENA
> *(HELENA holds out her hand expectantly to*
> *ARCHIMEDES, who reluctantly gives her the ball, which*
> *she then tosses to ERATOSTHENES. The children go off to*
> *play. She looks up sternly at her husband.)*
Medion, dearest, I know how important these cunning sections are to you, but…

ARCHIMEDES
Conic sections.

HELENA
Whatever they are called! Why don't you leave your precious geometry for a while and *play* with the children just for a change? They hardly ever see you!

ARCHIMEDES
I'm right here, aren't I?

HELENA
Are you?
(pause. No answer)
Well, are you?

ARCHIMEDES
(turning away)
I'm going to finish my...thought.

HELENA
Ugh! Phidias, you *must* speak to your son and talk some sense into him.
You are the only one here that he will listen to.

PHIDIAS
It's alright, Helena dear. Don't get upset.

HELENA
Will you talk to him?

PHIDIAS
Yes, of course I will. Go back to your weaving.

HELENA
Thank you, Papa. Tiberius, will you help Phidias up to the roof? Come, children.

> *(She kisses PHIDIAS on the forehead, then leads the
> children indoors. ARÊTE and CORNELIA follow. TIBERIUS
> crosses to PHIDIAS, helps him stand up, then escorts the
> old man to the second floor.)*

TIBERIUS
Give me your arm... there we go... gently now...there.

> *(ARCHIMEDES looks up from his sand-board, sees his
> father.)*

ARCHIMEDES
Papa!

PHIDIAS
Help me sit down.

ARCHIMEDES
I suppose you've come to tell me I was wrong to be upset with the children.

PHIDIAS
Well, they are children, Medion. You were once, too. Remember?

ARCHIMEDES
I know, Papa. I'm sorry.

PHIDIAS
What were you working on?

ARCHIMEDES
This? Well, it's the same problem I told you about last week.

PHIDIAS
The volume of the sphere?

ARCHIMEDES
I was so close to the answer, Papa. You know how that feels, don't you?

PHIDIAS
I do. There is no other feeling in the world like it.

ARCHIMEDES
So close, and then...this.

PHIDIAS
(looking at the ball on the sand-board, slightly amused)
The ball landed perfectly in the middle of your circle.

ARCHIMEDES
As if the children had aimed it there. It fits perfectly.

> *(They both stare at the large ball sitting in the sand-box.*
> *They laugh. ARCHIMEDES sighs.)*

I wish Helena understood me better. I try to explain my thoughts to her, but she just gets annoyed and says "I'm busy now." She thinks I'm absent-minded.

PHIDIAS
Well, you are, aren't you?

ARCHIMEDES
I suppose...No, not really.

(HELENA emerges from the house below and sings her
solitary thoughts in tune with ARCHIMEDES.)

ARCHIMEDES
    PEOPLE CALL ME ABSENT-MINDED,
    THEY DON'T UNDERSTAND
    I'M JUST PRESENT IN ANOTHER PLACE.
    THEY JUST NOD WITH KNOWING SMILES, YES,
    THERE HE GOES AGAIN:
    THEY'RE NOT PRESENT IN THAT OTHER PLACE.

    IF THEY ONLY KNEW THE TREASURES
    WAITING TO BE FOUND
    IN THAT PLACE WHERE COMMON SENSE CAN'T GO,
    THEY WOULD KNOW UNEARTHLY PLEASURES
    OF THE MIND UNBOUND
    FROM THE SHIFTING SEMBLANCES BELOW.

    IN THAT PLACE I FEEL AT HOME
    AS SURELY AS TO THIS;
    I AM CAPTIVE TO THE FREEDOM THERE.
    OTHERS I WOULD TAKE THERE WITH ME
    IF IT WERE THEIR WISH;
    ALL I SEE ARE UNBELIEVING STARES.

HELENA
    I DON'T MIND HE'S ABSENT-MINDED,
    I WOULD ONLY ASK
    THAT HE SPEND A MOMENT HERE WITH ME.
    TAKE SOME THOUGHT FOR THOSE WHO MIND HIM,
    LOOK UP FROM HIS TASK
    AND ALLOW HIMSELF TO BE WITH ME.

    ARCHIMEDES, HARKEN TO ME,
    HARKEN TO YOUR WIFE,
    HARKEN TO THE ONE WHO CARES FOR THEE,
    PAUSE TO TAKE A LOOK AT THOSE
    WHOSE WORK SUSTAINS YOUR LIFE;
    PAUSE TO LOOK AT LONG-FORGOTTEN ME.

GO ON BEING ABSENT-MINDED,
JOURNEY WHERE YOU MAY,
I SHALL ALWAYS BE HERE AT YOUR SIDE.
STILL, I HOPE YOU'LL NOT BE BLIND,
YOU'LL HEAR ME WHEN I PRAY
THAT OUR LIVES WILL SOMEDAY COINCIDE.

ARCHIMEDES
IN THE DISTANT LAND OF EGYPT
THERE'S A PLACE I KNOW;
I AM NOT A STRANGER IN THAT LAND.
HOW I LONG TO BOARD A SHIP
AND WATCH THE ROWERS ROW
TO THE CITY ALEXANDER PLANNED.

ARCHIMEDES and *HELENA*
ALEXANDRIA, ALEXANDRIA,
Archimedes,
LET ME PLEASE RETURN,
Won't you please return,
LET ME BREATHE THE MAGIC OF YOUR AIR.
Won't you find a time for us to share.
LET ME SEE YOUR BEACON SHINE
Let me see your beacon smile
ONCE MORE ACROSS THE SEA,
Once more when you see me,
LET ME FIND THE FRIENDS I ONCE KNEW THERE.
Let me find the friend I once knew there.
THERE WE ALL WERE ABSENT-MINDED
Go on being absent-minded,
BUT WE UNDERSTOOD
I will understand,
WE WERE PRESENT IN THAT OTHER PLACE.
You are present in that other place.
NO ONE STARED AND NO ONE MINDED,
I won't stare and I won't mind it,
FOR IT WAS OUR TASK
But of thee I ask,
TO BE PRESENT IN THAT OTHER PLACE.
You be present in this other place.
                    (HELENA exits)

PHIDIAS
(pause)
You miss Alexandria, don't you?

ARCHIMEDES
(sighing)
I do, Papa. There I had colleagues – no, *friends* – who understood me. And I understood them! They were fellow travelers. Papa, my friend Eratosthenes discovered the circumference of the *Earth*! Yet hardly set foot outside Alexandria. He didn't need to. He did it with his *mind*! I miss him.

PHIDIAS
You have another Eratosthenes now. Your own son. You must teach him your friend's discovery. Who knows, maybe if you teach him well, he will be able to join you in your journeys of the mind.

ARCHIMEDES
Do you think so, Papa?

PHIDIAS
(smiling)
I taught you, didn't I?

ARCHIMEDES
(*smiling and embracing his father)*
You did, Papa. Thank you.

SCENE 5

SETTING: (In the palace of HIERON, king of Syracuse. HIERON confers with
his chief minister, LEPTINES. They are studying a map of the
Mediterranean together)

HIERON
What news, Leptines? Are our Roman *friends* satisfied with our behavior?

LEPTINES
My spies tell me that Rome is happy and contented, King Hieron.

HIERON
(He points at map accordingly with what follows.)
She should be, having gorged herself on Corsica and Sardinia at Carthage's expense.
This map grows redder with each new Roman conquest.

LEPTINES
And Carthaginian green keeps shrinking.

HIERON
And how does *Carthage* fare?

LEPTINES
She chafes under Rome's bit. She expects obedience of others, not herself.

HIERON
What news of Hamilcar?

LEPTINES
He is busy establishing a new Carthage in Spain. Word has it that he swears
vengeance on Rome.

HIERON
How soon?

LEPTINES
It will take him years, perhaps decades, to build the necessary strength.

HIERON
I wouldn't underestimate that African lion...I met him once, you know; looked into
his eyes.

LEPTINES
What did you see?

HIERON
A furnace of hatred for all things Roman.

LEPTINES
Well, he's no threat to us.

HIERON
I wouldn't be so sure. If he has his way, Carthage will rise again, and rise for one purpose only - to destroy Rome. And if that happens – no, *when* that happens – Syracuse will be caught once again in the middle.
            (He sees ARCHIMEDES.)
Ah, but here comes my guest. We shall speak more of this later.

            *(LEPTINES departs as PHILISTIS, HIERON's wife and
            ARCHIMEDES' sister, enters leading ARCHIMEDES,
            ERATOSTHENES, and GELON, HIERON's son. GELON
            is holding a mechanical toy. Both boys are absorbed in its
            wonders. HIERON approaches ARCHIMEDES in warm
            welcome.)*

Archimedes, welcome! I trust your family is well?

ARCHIMEDES
Thank you, lordship, my wife and mother are well.

HIERON
And your father?

ARCHIMEDES
He is...he is old. It is not easy for him.

HIERON
You must tell me the moment there is a problem. I will send my own doctor. You will do that, won't you?

ARCHIMEDES
I will.

HIERON
He taught me once, you know?

ARCHIMEDES
He did? He never told me.

HIERON
I was *not* a very good student. Perhaps he was protecting me. Your father is a kind man and an excellent teacher.

ARCHIMEDES
Thank you, my lord. May I ask...?

GELON
(He has been tugging impatiently at his father's clothes.)
Papa, look at the toy catapult Uncle Archimedes brought me.

HIERON
Now, Gelon, have I not taught you not to interrupt when the grown-ups are speaking to one another?

GELON
Yes, Papa, sorry.

HIERON
Oh, but I see what you mean. It *is* a wonderful toy.

GELON
Look, Papa, I'll show you how it works.
                    (He demonstrates the use of the catapult.)

HIERON
(clapping and pointing to place where the ammunition strikes)
Bravo! Is that where you were aiming?

GELON
Exactly where I was aiming, Papa.

HIERON
One day you will command a real army with such weapons, Gelon.

GELON
Will I really, Papa?

HIERON
Yes, really! Did you thank your uncle?

GELON
Thank you, Uncle Archimedes.

ARCHIMEDES
You're most welcome, Gelon.

HIERON
Now, you and Eratosthenes run along and play, and I will see you later.

PHILISTIS
Say good-bye to your fathers, boys.

GELON AND ERATOSTHENES
Good-bye, Papa. Good bye, Uncle.

(PHILISTIS departs with the boys.)

HIERON
Now, what were you going to ask me?

ARCHIMEDES
I was wondering why you asked me here?

HIERON
That catapult, could you design others like it to defend our city?

ARCHIMEDES
But Syracuse already has catapults. Plenty of them.

HIERON
Yes, but not like the ones I suspect that you could design.
Could you make bigger and better ones?

ARCHIMEDES
Yes, of course, as bigger and better as you wish.

HIERON
As bigger and better...That's a bold claim.

ARCHIMEDES
Once you understand the principle, you know there are no theoretical limits
to these machines.

HIERON
Explain.

ARCHIMEDES
GIVE ME A PLACE TO STAND ON;
GIVE ME SUFFICIENT BERTH;
GIVE ME A LEVER STRONG AS IT IS LONG
AND I WILL MOVE THE EARTH.

CHORUS
GIVE HIM A PLACE TO STAND ON;
GIVE HIM SUFFICIENT BERTH;
GIVE HIM A LEVER STRONG AS IT IS LONG
AND HE WILL MOVE THE EARTH.

ARCHIMEDES
GIVE ME A FEW ROUND PULLEYS;
GIVE ME SOME ROPE UNFURLED;
LET ME ARRANGE THEM JUST AS I SEE FIT
AND I WILL MOVE THE WORLD.

CHORUS
GIVE HIM A FEW ROUND PULLEYS;
GIVE HIM SOME ROPE UNFURLED;
LET HIM ARRANGE THEM JUST AS HE SEES FIT
AND IIE WILL MOVE THE WORLD.

ARCHIMEDES
IF YOU WISH TO GAIN ADVANTAGE
OVER EARTHLY LOADS,
BE WILLING TO EXTEND YOUR EFFORTS
OVER LONGER ROADS;
YOU WILL EASE YOUR BURDEN BY JUST
FOLLOWING THIS CODE;
TRUST ME WHEN I TELL YOU THAT IT'S TRUE.

CHORUS
> TRUST HIM WHEN HE TELLS YOU THIS IS TRUE.

ARCHIMEDES
> GIVE ME A WHEEL AND AXLE;
> GIVE ME A WEDGE AND SCREW;
> GIVE ME AN INCLINED PLANE TO SCURRY UP
> THIS WORLD I'LL MOVE FOR YOU.

CHORUS
> GIVE HIM A WHEEL AND AXLE;
> GIVE HIM A WEDGE AND SCREW;
> GIVE HIM AN INCLINED PLANE TO SCURRY UP
> THIS WORLD HE'LL MOVE FOR YOU!

HIERON
(laughing)
You've convinced me. But I'm not asking you to move the earth. How about rocks of the size we used to build the walls of Syracuse?

ARCHIMEDES
That should not be difficult. But why? We are at peace. We have nothing to fear. We enjoy the protection of Rome.

HIERON
We enjoy the protection of Rome only as long as Rome sees fit to protect us. And Rome *will* continue to protect us if I have anything to say about it.

ARCHIMEDES
Then why do you need me to make catapults for you?

HIERON
Archimedes, none of us live forever. I cannot guarantee that my successor will uphold the alliance with Rome. *Things change*! Surely you must see that. I love Syracuse, and I would do everything in my power to protect it...beyond the grave if I could. Wouldn't you do the same?
> (*ARCHIMEDES is silent.*)
Ah, still thinking about going back to Alexandria, are you?

ARCHIMEDES
Yes.

HIERON
Why should the King of Egypt have first claim on your ability? You're a Syracusan, not an Alexandrian.

ARCHIMEDES
I know, but...

HIERON
Look, Archimedes, I can't and I won't try to force you to do this for your city. You are my brother-in-law, and besides, I'm not sure I *could* make you do something against your will, even if I tried. But I want you to think about your family. How happy do you think *they* would be in Alexandria? Have you thought about that?

ARCHIMEDES
It would be difficult at first, I'm sure.

HIERON
Difficult. Hmmm, you are a brilliant man, Archimedes. I know that. But I don't think you've thought this through very clearly.

ARCHIMEDES
I...perhaps...if you could just...

HIERON
(patting ARCHIMEDES on the shoulder)
You don't have to make up your mind all at once. You're right. Syracuse *is* at peace, and doesn't need to fear for the time being. Take your time. Will you think it over?

ARCHIMEDES
Yes, I will. Is that all?

HIERON
Yes.
                    (ARCHIMEDES proceeds to depart.)
Wait! I have something to show you. Leptines?

LEPTINES
Lordship?

HIERON
Leptines, bring the crown in here, will you?

LEPTINES
At once, lordship.

*(He enters bearing a gold crown. He hands it to HIERON
who then shows it to ARCHIMEDES.)*

HIERON
I ordered this crown made for me several weeks ago. I gave the goldsmith a carefully weighed lump of gold from which to craft the crown.

(HIERON hands the crown to ARCHIMEDES, who studies it.)

ARCHIMEDES
I see. It looks like fine workmanship.

HIERON
Oh, the workmanship is excellent, no doubt. But that's not the problem. You see I just can't be sure it's made *only* of the pure gold I gave the goldsmith.

ARCHIMEDES
You think it's been alloyed with a baser metal - like silver?

HIERON
Well, I can't be sure, but I have a sense for these things, you know. The goldsmith swears up and down he hasn't cheated me, but...well, how can I be sure? Do you know a way?

ARCHIMEDES
No, not off-hand.

HIERON
Do you think you could come up with a way to be sure?...Without destroying the crown?

ARCHIMEDES
I could try, I suppose.

HIERON
Would you?

ARCHIMEDES
I can't promise.

HIERON
Just try. Could you give me an answer in two weeks time?
I have an affair of state that requires the crown.

ARCHIMEDES
I will try, lordship. May I take the crown with me?

HIERON
You may.

ARCHIMEDES
Am I free to go now?

HIERON
You are. Please give my warmest regards to your parents. I wish you joy.

ARCHIMEDES
I wish you joy.
                (bows and exits)

LEPTINES
Did he agree to your proposal, Lordship?

HIERON
About the crown? Yes, he'll come up with a solution, I'm sure of it.

LEPTINES
No, I mean about the weapons.

HIERON
Oh! No.

LEPTINES
Ungrateful man! Why can't you order him to do the work?

HIERON
Order Archimedes? What, and have him fly off to Alexandria at the first opportunity?

LEPTINES
But you are the king. He *must* obey you.

HIERON
(pause)
Leptines, have you ever heard the story of Daedalus?

LEPTINES
The one who crafted wings for himself and his son? Icarus, wasn't it?
The one who flew too close to the sun?

HIERON
Yes.

LEPTINES
The father – Daedalus - survived, didn't he?

HIERON
He escaped to freedom on this very island of Sicily.

LEPTINES
Freedom?

HIERON
He was fleeing from the king who employed him – Minos of Crete.

LEPTINES
So…you think Alexandria…

HIERON
I'm not about to repeat Minos' mistake. Archimedes must learn by himself where his
heart belongs, and I will give him all the time he needs.

SCENE 6

SETTING: (The courtyard of ARCHIMEDES' home. ARCHIMEDES is on the second floor again, but this time he is staring fixedly at the crown. In the courtyard sits a screen blocking the view of the bathtub. CORNELIA and TIBERIUS are busy bringing water in buckets to fill it. HELENA emerges from a room looking worried. She glances at the sundial (or sun).

HELENA
Look at the time! Archimedes is due at the palace within the hour!
Has he bathed yet?

TIBERIUS
Every time I mention it he says, "Just give me a moment, Tiberius,
just give me a moment."

HELENA
(to CORNELIA)
Did you wash his chiton?

CORNELIA
(holding up the chiton)
Right here, mistress. Clean as a whistle.

HELENA
Thank goodness for that!
(calling up to ARCHIMEDES)
Medion, you've got to come down and bathe! Your appointment with Hieron will not
wait, do you hear me?

ARCHIMEDES
I just need a few moments more.

HELENA
(about to lose her temper, then speaking to CORNELIA)
Is the bath ready?

CORNELIA
Almost full, mistress.

HELENA
Finish filling the bathtub. Right now! Alright, Tiberius, I know he's your master, and you shouldn't lay a finger on him, but *I'm* giving you permission to take that man – by force, if necessary. Bring him downstairs.

(TIBERIUS raises his hands in protest.)

I don't care if he screams at you – and force him into that bathtub. Do you hear me?

TIBERIUS
Y-yes, mistress. As you wish.

HELENA
You have him down here in the next minute.
(takes deep breath)
All right. Water for the bath.

> *(She helps CORNELIA. TIBERIUS ascends the stairs and approaches ARCHIMEDES, back turned to him, hesitantly.)*

TIBERIUS
Master, I...

ARCHIMEDES
(fending him off with a gesture)
I know, I know. Just a few minutes more...

TIBERIUS
Forgive me master, I mean no harm.

> *(He wrestles ARCHIMEDES to his feet and forces him down the staircase.)*

ARCHIMEDES
Eh? What's this? Let me go! Take your hands off me!

> *(What follows can be heard, but not seen, as ARCHIMEDES is taken behind the screen.)*

HELENA
Right. Take off your chiton!

ARCHIMEDES
Helena, wait!

HELENA
Tiberius, Cornelia, help me take this man's chiton OFF!

>	*(TIBERIUS and CORNELIA disappear behind the screen. There are sounds of struggle and protest.)*

There! Now! Get in the bathtub!

ARCHIMEDES
It's full to the brim!

HELENA
I don't care. Get in the tub!

ARCHIMEDES
Look, I only need a few more…

HELENA
Tiberius, Cornelia, help me get this grown man into the bathtub!

ARCHIMEDES
Alright! Alright! I'll get in. Give me some room, please.

HELENA
You can have as much room as you need. Just get in.

>	*(There is the sound of stirring and dripping water and a long enough pause to allow for ARCHIMEDES to immerse himself and experience his epiphany.)*

ARCHIMEDES
Ooh, the water's hot.

HELENA
GET IN!

ARCHIMEDES
Ooh…aaaaah! That's nice.

HELENA
Tiberius, wash him.

TIBERIUS
Yes, mistr—

ARCHIMEDES
Wait! look at that! I get in, and the water...did you see that, Helena?

HELENA
See what? Start scrubbing him, Tiberius.

ARCHIMEDES
Wait! The water's overflowing, don't you see? We just have to collect it.

HELENA
Collect it? What on earth...?

ARCHIMEDES
Yes, that's it! Tiberius, get some more water! Refill the bathtub to the brim!
I'm getting out!

HELENA
Oh, no you don't! Get back in right now! Tiberius...?

ARCHIMEDES
No, stop! Don't you see? We just have to collect the water! Eureka! I've got it!

HELENA
Got what? Have you gone mad?

ARCHIMEDES
Success! I've got it!

> (ARCHIMEDES tries to run away, but HELENA races to
> block his movement. Blocked one way, ARCHIMEDES tries
> to escape in the other direction, as HELENA races to stop
> him. TIBERIUS and CORNELIA carry the screen to block
> the view of ARCHIMEDES. A frantic conversation ensues
> between all four as the mad pursuit takes place.)

HELENA	ARCHIMEDES	TIBERIUS	CORNELIA
I don't understand.			
	Eureka!		
		Master!	
			Grab him!
Stop!			
	Collect the water!		
		That way!	
			Oh dear!

(ARCHIMEDES sprawls to the ground, looks up, and sees HELENA blocking his path. He gets up slowly, looking at her warily, appears to have come to his senses; then as HELENA relaxes he bolts off stage.)

HELENA
Medion! Put some clothes on! Tiberius follow him! Bring him back! Zeus, my husband's gone mad!

TIBERIUS
Master! Come back! I've got your clothes here!

(We catch glimpses of ARCHIMEDES running across the back of the stage and through the audience, as TIBERIUS chases him through the streets of Syracuse. The music strikes up as the people of Syracuse come forth to sing.)

TOWNSPEOPLE
DID YOU SEE WHAT I JUST SAW
FLASH IN FRONT OF ME?
TELL ME OR I'LL NOT BELIEVE MY EYES.
YES, I SAW, I THINK I SAW,
WHAT YOU SAY YOU SAW,
I'VE A FEELING WE'VE BEEN SCANDALIZED.

EUREKA! EUREKA!
I THINK I SAW A STREAKER
A-RUNNING THROUGH THE STREETS
AS WE NOW SPEAK.
HE'S GOT IT! HE'S GOT IT!
I KNOW IT'S AWFULLY HOT YET,
HIS CLOTHES HE HAS FORGOT;
I'M GETTING WEAK.

44

I JUST SAW A MAN SPEEDING
NAKED THROUGH THE STREETS,
NOT A STITCH OF CLOTHING ON HIS BACK.
WAS IT ARCHIMEDES,
WITH NOTHING ON HIS FEET?
YOU WOULD THINK AT LEAST HE'D WEAR A SACK.

EUREKA! EUREKA!
I THINK I SAW A STREAKER
A-RUNNING THROUGH THE STREETS
AS WE NOW SPEAK.
HE'S GOT IT! HE'S GOT IT!
I KNOW IT'S AWFULLY HOT YET,
HIS CLOTHES HE HAS FORGOT;
I'M GETTING WEAK!

LOOK WHERE HE IS HEADING TO,
SURELY THIS CANNOT BE TRUE!
LOOK, HE'S STANDING AT THE PALACE GATE!
THERE'S A GUARD ARRESTING HIM!
CHANCES ARE HIS CAPER'S THROUGH;
IN THE PRISON HE WILL HAVE TO WAIT.

EUREKA! EUREKA!
I THINK I SAW A STREAKER
A-RUNNING THROUGH THE STREETS
AS WE NOW SPEAK.
HE'S GOT IT! HE'S GOT IT!
I KNOW IT'S AWFULLY HOT YET,
HIS CLOTHES HE HAS FORGOT;
I'M GETTING WEAK!

EUREKA!

SCENE 7

SETTING: (Hieron's palace)

PHINEAS
(pleading)
King Hieron, I served your predecessor, no less a man than Pyrrhus himself.
He trusted me.

HIERON
And perhaps he was right to do so. Or not. We will let Archimedes decide.

PHINEAS
Archimedes? The mechanic? What does he know of gold?

HIERON
Very little, I dare say. Nevertheless, he will decide.

PHINEAS
But why should a man who knows nothing of goldsmithing decide?

HIERON
Because *I* have decided that he will decide.
(to LEPTINES, impatient)
Where is that man anyway?

>   *(LEPTINES shrugs as PHILISTIS enters with a distraught*
>   *HELENA, TIBERIUS, CORNELIA, and a court servant.*
>   *PHILISTIS whispers to HIERON.)*

He did what? *(whisper)* Through the streets? *(whisper)* No clothes!?! *(whisper)*
Where is he now? *(whisper)* In prison? *(whisper. PHILISTIS holds forth a scrolled*
note.) Let me see it.

>   *(HIERON reads the note, then looks at no one in*
>   *particular.)*

By Zeus, what will this man do next!? Leptines!

LEPTINES
Lordship?

HIERON
Go to the prison. You'll find Archimedes there. Bring him here immediately.
No, wait! Put some clothes on him first.

LEPTINES
At once, lordship.
(bow and exit)

HIERON
(turning to the servant, and handing him the note)
Here is a list of Archimedes' requests. See that they are carried out.

SERVANT
As you wish, my lord.
(bow and exit)

PHINEAS
(sensing opportunity)
Majesty, is something wrong?

HIERON
Nothing that concerns you! Wait over there!

(PHINEAS bows, retreats to the edge of the room.)

HELENA
(upset, imploringly)
King Hieron, you must forgive Archimedes. He was bathing, getting ready to see
you when...I don't know what came into him. He got so excited, he ran out into the
street...
(She bursts into tears)
                    ...without any clothes on!

PHILISTIS
There, there, sister. Calm yourself.

HELENA
He sometimes just forgets himself. He does that, you know.

HIERON
I know.

HELENA
(gesturing to TIBERIUS who carries ARCHIMEDES' chiton)
I have his clothes here.

HIERON
That won't be necessary. Philistis, dear, why don't you sit Helena down.

PHILISTIS
(leading HELENA to a seat, and sitting next to her, holding her hand)
Come with me, Helena. Everything will be alright. You'll see.

> (Two servants return, having brought with them the
> objects ARCHIMEDES had requested: two equal-sized
> copperpots, sitting in two copper basins, a large pitcher
> of water, two equal-sized glass vessels, and wooden box.
> They arrange them on a table (forestage) such that the
> audience can see the two pot/basin assemblies next to
> each other, with one glass vessel next to each pot/basin.
> They pour (imaginary) water to the brim of each pot.
> Everyone looks on with interest.)

SERVANT
To your satisfaction, lordship?

HIERON
That's what his directions say.

> (He nods, and the servants retire to the entrance, just as
> LEPTINES returns with a now fully clad ARCHIMEDES.)

HELENA
(getting up and rushing towards ARCHIMEDES)
Medion, how could you have done this! You've made a laughing-stock of us...

PHILISTIS
(gently redirecting HELENA back to her seat)
There, there, sister, it's alright. Come, let's see what Archimedes has prepared for us.

ARCHIMEDES
(in a state of shock)
Lordship, I...you see I...I didn't mean to...

HIERON
(in no rush, amused at ARCHIMEDES' embarrassment)
Did you...solve my problem?

ARCHIMEDES
Your problem? I'm sorry, what prob...? Oh! Your problem! Yes, I know the answer. I mean if you brought the things I asked for, we can find out the answer.

HIERON
Very well, proceed.

ARCHIMEDES
Yes! It's really quite simple. Now, let's see here. Yes, these pots look to be equal in size, and they are both full to the brim. Where is the gold?

>   *(He sees it in the box, lifts it out, and displays it*
>   *for all to see.)*

Ah! Here it is! Is it exactly the same weight as the gold lump you gave to the goldsmith?

HIERON
It is. Wouldn't you agree, Phineas? Come and take a look.

>   *(PHINEAS approaches, none too eagerly, and inspects the*
>   *lump of gold.)*

PHINEAS
Close enough, I suppose. But what's this got to do...?

HIERON
Phineas the goldsmith meet Archimedes the...mechanic. Now, Archimedes, be so kind as to demonstrate.

ARCHIMEDES
Right! Well, you see if we lower the original weight of gold into one vessel, and the crown into the other, they should displace an equal volume of water, right?

HIERON
That makes sense, yes. But...where is the crown?

ARCHIMEDES
Yes, now for the crown!
(suddenly horror-struck)
Oh no! I forgot to bring the crown!

TIBERIUS
(strides forward and lifts up the chiton to reveal the crown)
Is this what you are looking for, master?

ARCHIMEDES
Oh, Tiberius, you've saved the day! I can't thank you enough!

> (He can't decide whether to take the crown from
> TIBERIUS, or to hug him.)

TIBERIUS
(gesturing towards HIERON)
Master?

ARCHIMEDES
What?...Oh! Yes, of course, the experiment. Let's see, where were we? Oh, yes. Now Tiberius, you lower the crown gently into this vessel, and I'll do the same with this lump over here. Ready?

> (They each lower their respective objects slowly into the
> copper pots.)

You see how the water is being displaced into the basins below? Now, let's compare the volumes of the displaced water. Tiberius, do as I do.

> (They empty the contents of each basin into the glass jars.
> ARCHIMEDES holds them up to display their imagined
> contents.)

There! You see, the water displaced by the crown is clearly more than the water displaced by the lump of gold, which means...

HIERON
(slowly turning towards PHINEAS, who is slowly edging to the exit)
Which means that somebody has been cheating the king! Not so fast!

> (PHINEAS is captured and held by the two servants)
Well, Phineas, do you know what the penalty is for stealing the king's gold?

PHINEAS
Oh, my lord, I beg mercy. It was a mistake, I assure you. I don't know how it happened. No, wait, it must have been my assistant. Oh, just wait till I get my hands on him.

HIERON
That will be quite enough, Phineas. Leptines, see that he's taken to a cell, and notify the executioner.

(LEPTINES nods to HIERON, then to the servants, who lead PHINEAS, now weeping, away.)

PHINEAS
Lordship, I have a wife, and children...

(ARCHIMEDES is visibly concerned.)

ARCHIMEDES
King Hieron, I did not know I would be the cause of another man's death. Is it really nec...

HIERON
Such matters must be dealt with firmly and according to the ancient custom. You must think of it no further. Now, you have done me a great service. How can I reward you? Anything at all.

ARCHIMEDES
Lordship, I do not wish for a reward. Not after...anything at all?

HIERON
You only need ask.

ARCHIMEDES
I would like that goldsmith to perform a service for me.

HIERON
I'm sorry, Archimedes, ask me for gold, ask me for silver, ask me for anything but this.

ARCHIMEDES
I thought you said anything.

HIERON
There is the law, Archimedes. I must uphold it.

ARCHIMEDES
(gestures to depart)
Very well. Helena.

HIERON
Wait! You're right, I did say anything, and what good is a king's word if he cannot keep it. You may have your wish. Say on.

ARCHIMEDES
I wish this goldsmith to design a sphere and a cylinder. Copper will do. But it must be to my exact specifications, and…

HIERON
And?

ARCHIMEDES
And if he performs the task to my satisfaction, that he be allowed to live and support his family.

HIERON
You have my word.

SCENE 8

SETTING: (ARCHIMEDES' home. ARCHIMEDES'and TIBERIUS' entire families sit together in the courtyard. They have been enjoying themselves with food and drink. There is laughter as TIBERIUS is in the middle of a story. The three children sit together not quite knowing what to think, but they laugh when the adults laugh)

TIBERIUS
(barely able to get his words out, he is laughing so hard)
You should have seen the look on Kallicrates' eyes as Archimedes streaked by him. They were wider than saucers. He dropped the two melons he was carrying to the pavement. Splat! All over his wife's tunic. And then, and then, his wife called out to her children, "Children, children, hide your eyes!" and she gathered them into the folds of her tunic.

(laughter all around, including ARCHIMEDES')

HELENA
Oh dear, and I shall never forget the look on Medion's face when he discovered he'd forgotten the crown. "Yes, the crown...oh no!" Oh, Medion, you looked so forlorn!

ARCHIMEDES
If truth be told, I wished I could get back in the bathtub.

PHIDIAS
(as the laughter settles)
But your solution worked. Hieron must have been very impressed.

ARCHIMEDES
Yes, but Papa, there's so much more to it than that. I think I have discovered a principle, one that all floating and sinking objects obey.

PHIDIAS
Yes?

ARÊTE
(seeing HELENA's face darken, putting her hand on PHIDIAS' arm)
No, Phidias, dear, let's not talk about it tonight.

ARCHIMEDES
Mama's right. Tonight we should celebrate. Let's make some music together.

ALL SING
ON THIS ISLAND OF THE SUN,
WHERE PERSEPHONE ASCENDS TO MEET HER MOTHER ONCE AGAIN;
AND THE FACE OF SPRING SHINES BRIGHTLY
AS ACROSS THE MEADOWS SPRIGHTLY
TO HER MOTHER SHE DOES RUN;
TO THE WAITING ARMS OF DEMETER,
HER WINTER TIME OF SAD LAMENT
AND SORROW OVERCOME,
AND THE WILL OF ZEUS IS DONE
ON THIS ISLAND OF THE SUN.

ON THIS ISLAND OF THE SUN,
WHERE HEPHAESTUS STOKES THE FURNACE OF HIS SMITHY UNDERGROUND;
AND THE BOWELS OF AETNA RUMBLE
WITH THE LIGHTNING AND THE THUNDER
OF HIS HAMMER AND HIS MIND;

AS HE LABORS TO RECOVER
FROM OUTRAGES THAT HIS MOTHER
DID INFLICT UPON HER SON,
WHOSE DEFORMITY SHE SHUNNED,
ON THIS ISLAND OF THE SUN.

ON THIS ISLAND OF THE SUN,
WHERE ODYSSEUS SOUGHT REFUGE ON HIS WAND'RINGS FAR FROM HOME,
IT WAS HERE HE MET THE CYCLOPS
WHO QUITE NEARLY PUT A STOP
TO HIS HEROIC MARATHON;
AND THROUGH SCYLLA AND CHARYBDIS
HE SURVIVED ANOTHER CRISIS
WITH NARROW TWISTING RUN,
HIS HOMEWARD JOURNEY ALMOST DONE,
ON THIS ISLAND OF THE SUN.

ON THIS ISLAND OF THE SUN,
THERE'S A CITY MARRIED TO THE SEA I CALL MY VERY OWN;
WHERE THE SPRING OF ARETHUSA
EVER SINGS TO SYRACUSA
ON ITS BED OF MARBLED STONE;
AND THE EAR OF DIONYSUS
LISTENS TO THE FAR HORIZON
FOR THE SOUNDS OF DISTANT SONG,
ON THIS ISLAND, THIS ISLAND OF THE SUN.

> *(There is silence as everyone drinks in the peace and happiness of the night. HELENA rests her head on ARCHIMEDES' shoulder and strokes ERATOSTHENES' hair. TIBERIUS and CORNELIA rest theirs on LIVIA and LUCIUS. ARÊTE and PHIDIAS look on with contentment. HELENA breaks the silence.)*

HELENA
Eratosthenes, my olive, it's time for sleep. Come.
> *(She departs holding ERATOSTHENES' hand, nods to CORNELIA.)*

CORNELIA
Come Lucius, come Livia.
> *(She departs with TIBERIUS and the children.)*

54

ARÊTE
Phidi, my sweet, shall I help you to bed?

PHIDIAS
Not just yet, dear. I want to speak with Medion a little while.

ARÊTE
Not too late then. Good-night.

ARCHIMEDES
Good night, Mama. I'll help Papa to bed.

> (ARÊTE exits. There is silence as they gaze at the night
> sky together. There is a sudden and fleeting glow that
> interrupts their silence)

Did you see that, Papa?

PHIDIAS
Hephaestus is at work in the bowels of Aetna.
(looks up at sky and points)
There! Did you see that?

ARCHIMEDES
No?

PHIDIAS
A shooting star! The gods must be speaking to one another.

ARCHIMEDES
(pause)
Papa, I have something to ask you.

PHIDIAS
Ask.

ARCHIMEDES
You fell under Alexandria's spell when you were young, just like me. Why did you come back to Syracuse?

PHIDIAS
It was just a feeling at the time. I didn't really know why, not fully anyway.

ARCHIMEDES
What kind of feeling?

PHIDIAS
A feeling that *this* – Syracuse – was my home, where I belonged. My family, these limestone shores, Mount Aetna, the sea, the sound of music – *our* music.

ARCHIMEDES
But what about the Museum? The pursuit of knowledge with people eager to pursue it with you?

PHIDIAS
Look up. The sky is all I've ever really been interested in. Do you think the sky above Alexandria is any better than the sky above Syracuse?

ARCHIMEDES
Hmmm.
(pause)
Papa, I've made up my mind. I will stay. I could not be happy if Helena, Eratosthenes, you and Mama were not happy with me.

PHIDIAS
I am comforted.

ARCHIMEDES
Are you tired, Papa? Shall I help you to your bed?

PHIDIAS
No. Let's enjoy the night a little longer. No need to speak.

SCENE 9

SETTING: (In the dimly lit HIERON's palace. It is 40 years later. HIERON is very old and nearing death. Surrounding him are HIERONYMUS, his 15-year old grand-son, ADRANODORUS and DAMARATA, his son-in-law and daughter, who are also guardians to HIERONYMUS, PHILISTIS, ARCHIMEDES (now in his 70s) and HELENA, as well as attendants. Illuminated downstage, MARCELLUS resumes his conversation with LUCIA and LIVIA)

MARCELLUS
So Archimedes yielded to Hieron's persuasion and began to build his weapons?

LUCIUS
Yes, though never with his whole heart.

MARCELLUS
Why so?

LUCIUS
Master always said that geometry lifted his mind to…another place. And mechanics kept him here. I suppose he preferred the other place.

MARCELLUS
Why did Hieron choose to break the alliance with Rome?

LIVIA
Oh, but he did no such thing. It was that shameful grandson of his, Hieronymus.

LUCIUS
(spitting in disgust)
He brought disaster on everyone's head. I saw it with my own eyes.

MARCELLUS
Tell me what you saw.

LUCIUS
Master was summoned to the palace. You see, Hieron was close to death, and he wanted to set things right.

MARCELLUS
Go on.

*(Lights go up on HIERON's court as MARCELLUS and
the slaves depart. HIERONYMUS chatters idly with
DAMARATA and ADRANODORUS with a look of self-
satisfaction and contempt. HIERON sits on his throne,
obviously tired and depressed.)*

HIERON
Hieronymus, are you listening to me?

HIERONYMUS
(turning his gaze to his grandfather with deliberate laziness)
Of course I am listening to you, grandfather. To your every word.

HIERON
(ignoring the insult)
Good. You know I haven't much longer to live. When I die...

DAMARATA
May the gods forbid it.

HIERON
Be quiet. I'm going to die soon, and you know it. Hieronymus?

HIERONYMUS
Yes, dear grandfather.

HIERON
And don't "dear grandfather" me either. I know you're a young wretch, and you are
not fit to govern my city. Not yet, anyway. Look at you! You parade yourself in the
royal purple. Neither I nor your father ever flaunted our office so. You're insolent,
arrogant, and contemptuous towards your fellow citizens. You disregard the advice
of your elders. How do you expect to gain the trust of your people?

HIERONYMUS
Their fear and obedience will be quite sufficient.

HIERON
You'll have that, you can be sure. *And* their hatred.
(sighs)
Hieronymus, you must learn how to govern well and wisely. That's why I've
appointed your aunt and uncle here to act as your guardians.
> *(HIERONYMUS, DAMARATA, and ADRANODORUS
> smile at each other).*

And I've appointed others besides them – to keep an eye on you and them!
                    *(He stares accusingly at DAMARATA and
                    ADRANODORUS.)*

ADRANODORUS and DAMARATA *(overlapping)*
My Lord, your suspicions are unwarranted...
Father, how dare you...

HIERON
Stop your chatter. It's idle and you know it.
(with a hint of sorrow)
And I haven't any time left for it. I'll settle my affairs as I see fit.
(to HIERONYMUS)
Now what's all this I hear about you meeting with this Carthaginian envoy? Why are *you* meeting with him while *I* am still king?

HIERONYMUS
Grandfather, you have not been well. I do have some regard for you, you know. I intended to bring him before you...when you were well enough to receive him.

HIERON
Well, where is he?

HIERONYMUS
(to servant)
Bring Epikydes here before the king.

                    *(The servant departs and returns with EPIKYDES, who
                    bows deeply before HIERON.)*

HIERON
Who are you? What is your business here?

EPIKYDES
I am Epikydes of Carthage, my Lord, though my grandfather was born in Syracuse. I have fought these last few years in Hannibal's army. As I am sure you are aware, we have the Romans on the run. Rome is terrified.

HIERON
Terrified? Huh! Then what is Hannibal doing wasting his time in the south of Italy? Why doesn't he get on with it and finish the matter?

EPIKYDES
He is...gathering his strength to deliver the final blow. And that is why I am here, my Lord.

HIERON
You want me to help Hannibal to deliver the final blow?

EPIKYDES
You control territory vital to the interests of Rome...

HIERON
And Carthage.

EPIKYDES
Carthage has no wish to interfere with the interests of Syracuse, my Lord. She merely wishes that we advance our mutual interests.

HIERON
(getting up, advancing on EPIKYDES)
Listen. I "advanced mutual interests" with Carthage against Rome once long ago, and do you know what happened?

(EPIKYDES is silent.)

Cat got your tongue? Very well, I'll tell you what happened.

(to HIERONYMUS, who begrudgingly obeys)

And you listen, do you hear me? Carthage and Syracuse had allied against Rome, but when the Romans showed up, there was not a single Carthaginian to be seen. We bore the brunt of Rome's anger, but we survived - no thanks to Carthage! Since then Syracuse has enjoyed the benefit of fifty years of *faithful* alliance with Rome. So I wish you to take this message back to your master, Hannibal: with all due respect to his admirable fighting talents, I have absolutely no faith whatsoever that he will defeat Rome. Your master has bitten off far more than he can chew. And I – Syracuse – will not join him in his folly!

EPIKYDES
My Lord, you underestimate Hannibal...

60

HIERON
(to EPIKYDES)
 ENOUGH!
 YOU TAX MY PATIENCE AND MY MIND;
 I WARN YOU NOT TO TRY IT ANYMORE;
 YOU BLUFF!
 I SEE YOUR MOTIVE AND YOUR GAME;
 YOUR VERY PRESENCE HERE I DO ABHOR.
 BEGONE!
 YOU STAIN THE HONOR OF MY REALM;
 THE LABORS OF MY LIFE YOU WOULD DESTROY!
 AT ONCE!
 YOU THINK AN OLD MAN YOU'D DECEIVE;
 JUST AS YOU'VE TRICKED THIS PROUD AND FOOLISH BOY!

(to himself)
 HOW I WISH THE GODS WOULD GIVE ME STRENGTH AGAIN;
 HOW I YEARN TO CRUSH THEIR MAD DESIGNS;
 EVEN NOW THEY LAUGH TO HEAR ME THREATEN THEM,
 KNOWING HOW MY DAYS ARE IN DECLINE.

(to HIERONYMUS)
 AND YOU!
 YOU DISAPPOINT MY VERY SOUL;
 YOU HAVE NO THOUGHT FOR ANYONE BUT YOU!
 UNTRUE!
 YOU CHOOSE TO LIE AT EV'RY TURN;
 YOUR GREED AND LUST YOU'LL ONE DAY LEARN TO RUE.
 SUCH GALL!
 TO TREAT SO LIGHTLY YOUR DOMAIN,
 TO PLACE OUR CHERISHED HOME IN JEOPARDY;
 YOU'LL FALL!
 YOU MARK MY WORDS, YOU RECKLESS CHILD;
 YOUR PATH TO RUIN CLEARLY I FORESEE.

(to himself)
 HOW I WISH THE GODS WOULD GIVE ME STRENGTH AGAIN;
 HOW I YEARN TO CRUSH THEIR MAD DESIGNS;
 EVEN NOW THEY LAUGH TO HEAR ME THREATEN THEM,
 KNOWING HOW MY DAYS ARE IN DECLINE;
 HOW CLEAR IT IS, MY DAYS ARE IN DECLINE.

EPIKYDES
(angrily)
I shall inform Hannibal of your contempt for him. Do not expect mercy when Carthage is master of Italy!

> *(EPIKYDES departs angrily. HIERONYMUS follows. HIERON, exhausted, is shocked to see the latter's departure. ADRANODORUS and DAMARATA, after a little hesitation, also follow HIERONYMUS and EPIKYDES.)*

HIERON
Here! Where are you going?

> *(He is suddenly contorted with pain, moans, and seeks support)*

PHILISTIS
(rushing to his side)
Hieron, dear, are you alright?

HIERON
(sitting down, weakly)
It will pass.
(He pauses to gather his strength.)
Where is Archimedes? I want to talk to him. Quickly. I haven't long.

ARCHIMEDES
(approaching softly with HELENA at his side. He lays a hand on HIERON's arm as he sits down beside him.)
My Lord.

HIERON
How are you, my old friend?

ARCHIMEDES
I'm well, my Lord, but you mustn't…

HIERON
Have you solved your problem yet?

ARCHIMEDES
Problem?

HIERON
The volume of sphere. You didn't think I knew, did you? Or cared.

ARCHIMEDES
I had no idea.

HIERON
Listen to me, old friend. After I'm gone, few will remember me. But you?
The whole world will remember you.

ARCHIMEDES
My Lord, you will be remembered as the wisest of kings.

HIERON
I will be remembered as the king who was wise enough to give your talents a place
to flourish, and that is all.
(pause)
Archimedes, you saw what happened here. My grandson, he doesn't understand.
No, he *refuses* to understand! He may lead Syracuse into Carthage's hands, and if
that happens...Archimedes, will you promise me something?

ARCHIMEDES
Ask.

HIERON
Will you promise to defend Syracuse, no matter what?

ARCHIMEDES
I swear to do so.

HIERON
(relaxing, lying back)
Thank you. Philistis, I would hear music to soothe an aching heart. And I would lie
down.

> (PHILISTIS helps HIERON to lie down on a chaise
> which will become HIERON's deathbed, as the musical
> accompaniment to HIERON's "How I wish the gods..."
> begins. The music swells to a majesty befitting the passing
> of a great king.)

SCENE 10

SETTING: (The lights dim on the upstage palace scene as lights reveal MARCELLUS, LUCIUS, and LIVIA downstage. MARCELLUS resumes conversation with LUCIUS and LIVIA. As the mournful melody plays on, a sheet is drawn over HIERON's head to signify his death. He is carried off on his deathbed, followed by mourners which include all of the previous scene's participants. HIERONYMUS and EPIKYDES follow last, and peel off from the procession as it proceeds off-stage. According to the narrative indications which follow, HIERONYMUS and EPIKYDES each take turns sitting in the vacant throne)

MARCELLUS
And Archimedes remained firm to his oath to Hieron?

LIVIA
He did, Sir, and that despite his loathing for Hieronymus. He supervised the building of the defenses every day. He still does. But every day he laments the fact that we are fighting to defend ourselves against Rome. Hieron would never have let that happen.

MARCELLUS
What happened after Hieron died?

LUCIUS
His body had barely been placed in the tomb before Hieronymus had sealed an alliance with Carthage.

    (HIERONYMUS and EPIKYDES are seen to shake hands as these words are spoken. HIERONYMUS sits comfortably on the throne.)

MARCELLUS
What happened to Hieronymus?

LUCIUS
Exactly what Hieron predicted. The people quickly grew to hate him. They assassinated him.

    (HIERONYMUS exits.)

MARCELLUS
But how did Epikydes come to replace him?

LIVIA
He wouldn't have... if it hadn't been for you.

MARCELLUS
For me!?

LUCIUS
He reported your treatment of the Greek rebels at Leontini, how you ordered them all beaten to death.

MARCELLUS
I gave no such order! The only ones so treated were deserters from the Roman army. Not one Greek citizen was harmed.

LUCIUS
That's not what Epikydes said.

LIVIA
And the people of Syracuse believed him. That's when they elected him to lead us, and protect us...against Rome.

(EPIKYDES studies the throne, then sits down in it.)

MARCELLUS
It's a pity Hieron died when he did. Perhaps none of this would have been necessary.
(pause)
Would you save your master if you could?

LIVIA
How?

MARCELLUS
Tomorrow I will give the order for the attack to begin. It will not be a pretty sight. My soldiers have endured this siege for three years, and they have no such love for Syracuse as your master has – or as you appear to have. The slaughter will be cruel and bloody.

There is little I can do to prevent it. But I would have your master and his family live. They would have the promise of my protection...if we can find them before my army does. Could you lead the way to them?

LUCIUS and LIVIA *(overlapping)*
Aye, my lord. Yes, of course.

MARCELLUS
(to LIVIA)
No, not you. It will be far too dangerous for a woman.

(LIVIA is disappointed as MARCELLUS addresses LUCIUS.)

You will lead one of my soldiers to the house of Archimedes. He will escort all of you to safety outside the city. I warn you: for the next few days there will be *no* safety – for man, woman, or child – in the city. You must act swiftly, do you understand?

LUCIUS
Aye, my Lord.

MARCELLUS
Claudius!

(The scene ends as MARCELLUS gives instructions to CLAUDIUS, pointing out his intentions for LUCIUS.)

SCENE 11

SETTING: (One half of the stage represents the courtyard of ARCHIMEDES' house and the other represents street outside. In the courtyard ARCHIMEDES and ERATOSTHENES are opposite each other at ground level. CORNELIA stands apart cutting vegetables for a cooking vessel. From beyond the house we hear occasional indistinct shouts. ERATOSTHENES stands holding a copper sphere above a copper cylinder, apparently pouring something from the sphere into the cylinder. Then he shakes the sphere and holds his ear to it)

ERATOSTHENES
It's empty.

ARCHIMEDES
How full is the cylinder now?
(pause)
Just estimate.

ERATOSTHENES
Hmmm, maybe two thirds?

ARCHIMEDES
(handing him a measuring rod)
Measure it to be certain.

ERATOSTHENES
>*(He measures both the cylinder height and the depth of*
>*the water.)*

It is two thirds! Exactly two thirds!

ARCHIMEDES
Now you know.

ERATOSTHENES
I see, I see! The volume of the sphere must be… wait…wait…four thirds *pi r cubed*!

ARCHIMEDES
(smiling, standing and patting his son on the back)
You've got it! I'm very proud of you!

>*(During this conversation HELENA has entered and*
>*conferred silently with CORNELIA. CORNELIA gestures*
>*towards the vegetables, then to a large earthenware*
>*vessel off to the side. HELENA goes and looks in the vessel,*
>*looks up with some exasperation, and calls out*
>*to ARCHIMEDES.)*

HELENA
Medion, have you been using the water again for your experiments?

ERATOSTHENES
Mama, come see what Papa has just shown me.

HELENA
Not now, Eratosthenes. Medion, Cornelia is preparing our dinner and we don't have any water. What have you done with it?

ARCHIMEDES
(a little sheepishly, pointing to the cylinder)
It's in there.

HELENA
Bring it here, please.

ERATOSTHENES
I'll bring it, Mama. But first promise to come look.

HELENA
(with a touch of impatience)
Alright.

> *(ERATOSTHENES takes the cylinder to the cooking pot and empties the water into it. Then he returns to his father's side. CORNELIA immediately sets to work putting vegetables into the pot and stirring.)*

HELENA
(coming across and looking at the cylinder and sphere)
Aren't these the objects that that goldsmith made for you? The one who tried to cheat King Hieron? What was his name?

ARCHIMEDES
Phineas.

HELENA
What's become of him?

ARCHIMEDES
He left us many years ago. It was the same year that Tiberius passed.

HELENA
May Hades show him mercy.
(pause)
Tiberius, I mean. Imagine that: cheating the king. He should have been put to death...
Phineas, I mean.

ARCHIMEDES
(holding up the sphere and gazing at it)
Phineas did what I asked him to do. He did it well.

HELENA
Well, what have you two got to show me? Dinner's waiting.

ERATOSTHENES
Mama, we filled the sphere full with water, and...

HELENA
(looking suspiciously at the sphere)
Where?

ERATOSTHENES
(showing her the hole [it can be a black spot painted on the sphere])
Here, see?

HELENA
Oh. Go on then.

ERATOSTHENES
(He demonstrates as he speaks.)
Now the sphere fits exactly into this cylinder, you see? And the top of the sphere is level with the top of the cylinder.

HELENA
It's fine craftsmanship, I see that.

ERATOSTHENES
Yes, but then we poured the water into this cylinder. It fills exactly two thirds of the cylinder, do you see?

HELENA
So?

ERATOSTHENES
            *(looking at ARCHIMEDES for guidance. ARCHIMEDES
            gestures back as if to say, "It's in your hands now.")*
So...if you know how to find the volume of the cylinder, you know the volume of sphere, right?

HELENA
(exasperated)
What do you mean, if you know how to find the volume of the cylinder?
Tell me who knows such a thing.

ERATOSTHENES
Well, Papa does...and now I do.

HELENA
Very well, how do you find the volume of a cylinder?

ERATOSTHENES
Well…first of all you have to know the value of *pi*, then you…

HELENA
What do you mean, the value of pie? You think I don't feed you enough?

ERATOSTHENES
No, Mama, please, I only meant…you see, *pi* is a number.
(using the cylinder to gesture his meaning)
If you divide the circumference by the diameter, you get *pi*.
It's a bit bigger than three.

HELENA
How much bigger?

ERATOSTHENES
Well, that's the fascinating part, Mama. It's very close to one seventh more, but Papa says that we can never get exactly to the number, only closer and closer.

HELENA
And how does your Papa know this?

ARCHIMEDES
I trapped it.

HELENA
You trapped it. You trapped a number. Medion, you trap an animal, that I understand. Why would you trap a number?

ARCHIMEDES
Well, you wouldn't…normally. You'd only do it if the number was irrational.

HELENA
Irrational? Are you making fun of me? I'll tell you who's irrational….

ERATOSTHENES
Mama, Mama, Papa's only trying to say that if you know this number, finding the volume of the cylinder is as easy as…
(looking to ARCHIMEDES for the right expression)

HELENA	ERATOSTHENES	ARCHIMEDES
PIE?	*PI.*	*PI!*

ERATOSTHENES
    IT'S A REALLY SIGNIFICANT LETTER,

ARCHIMEDES
    AND I COULDN'T HAVE CHOSEN IT BETTER,

HELENA
    ALL I THINK OF IS SPINACH AND FETA
    BUT WHY FEEL THE LESSER FOR QUESTIONING.

HELENA	ERATOSTHENES	ARCHIMEDES
PIE?	PI.	PI!

ARCHIMEDES
    A COMPLETELY IRRATIONAL NUMBER

ERATOSTHENES
    AND IT SHOOK ME RIGHT OUT OF MY SLUMBER

HELENA
    IT JUST MAKES ME FEEL DUMBER AND DUMBER
    BUT THOSE TWO OUTNUMBER ME, SO I SEE

HELENA	ERATOSTHENES	ARCHIMEDES
PI.	PI.	PI!

HELENA
    IT'S A MYSTERY I SHOULD BE PRIZING

ERATOSTHENES
    AS A CONCEPT, IT'S QUITE HYPNOTIZING

ARCHIMEDES
    IS IT REALLY SO VERY SURPRISING
    WE BOTH COMPROMISE IN THE MATTER OF

HELENA	ERATOSTHENES	ARCHIMEDES
PI?	PIE.	PIE!

ARCHIMEDES
    IT'S DELICIOUS AND QUITE APPETIZING

ERATOSTHENES
    YES, YOUR COOKING IS WORTH ADVERTISING

HELENA
    OH, THE TWO OF YOU STOP BUTTERIZING
    AND START MEMORIZING THE VALUE OF
    TWO OF YOU STOP BUTTERIZING
    AND START MEMORIZING THE VALUE OF...

ERATOSTHENES
    LET'S THE TWO OF US STOP BUTTERIZING
    AND START MEMORIZING THE VALUE OF...

ARCHIMEDES
    LET'S THE...

HELENA, ERATOSTHENES and ARCHIMEDES *(in unison)*
    ...THREE OF US STOP BUTTERIZING
    AND START MEMORIZING THE VALUE OF
    PI, PI, PI!

> *(The three smile at each other and start laughing.
> The merriment is cut short by a scream from the city
> beyond. HELENA freezes.)*

HELENA
Did you hear that? Someone screamed.

ARCHIMEDES
Calm yourself, dear. It's just some foolish reveler who's had too much to drink. I shall be glad when this feast has ended.

HELENA
That didn't sound like revelry to me. Cornelia, did you hear that scream?

CORNELIA
Yes, mistress. It sounded like...someone in distress.

HELENA
Medion, Eratosthenes...perhaps you should see what the trouble is.

ARCHIMEDES
I have work to do. So do you. Go on about your business.

HELENA
(pausing for a moment, then shaking her head)
Perhaps you're right. Still…

> (She goes to help CORNELIA. ERATOSTHENES sits down
> once more with ARCHIMEDES, gazing at some figures he
> is drawing in the sand. On the street outside LUCIUS leads
> a Roman soldier named MARCUS to the door of the house.
> Shouts of soldiers and victims can be heard in thedistance.
> ARCHIMEDES and family continue their business unaware
> of what is going on outside.)

LUCIUS
This is the house.

MARCUS
Go inside and tell them why you're here. Tell them to get out here in a hurry. Don't bother to bring any precious belongings. Tell them they'll be lucky to live.

LUCIUS
Very well.
(He knocks on the door. ERATOSTHENES rises to and opens it.)

ERATOSTHENES
Lucius! How…?

LUCIUS
(entering swiftly and brushing by ERATOSTHENES. He addresses ARCHIMEDES and HELENA.)
Master, mistress, forgive me, but you must all get up and leave at once.

ARCHIMEDES
Lucius, what are you doing here? I thought you would be with…with your own people.

LUCIUS
(bowing to one knee before ARCHIMEDES)
Master, you are…no, there is no time for this. There is a soldier outside. He is here…

ARCHIMEDES
A soldier. What does Epikydes want now?

LUCIUS
No, master, a Roman soldier.

ARCHIMEDES
A Roman soldier. What is a Roman soldier doing...?

ERATOSTHENES
(who has grasped the situation now)
Papa, Mama, we must do as Lucius says. Don't you see, the Romans have breached the walls. We must go!

HELENA
Let me gather some things. Eratosthenes, Medion, quickly now.

LUCIUS
Marcus – I mean the soldier – said there isn't any time for it.

> *(But HELENA has already gone into a room, and so has ERATOSTHENES. ARCHIMEDES merely looks down at his work and continues his train of thought. LUCIUS raises his hands in resignation.*
>
> *Meanwhile, MARCUS paces back and forth outside, obviously impatient. Two Roman soldiers, looking drunk and bloodthirsty, run by and stop when they see MARCUS. Each one is carrying a precious object.)*

BRAXUS
Marcus, what are you up to? Not enjoying yourself? Come and join the fun!

MARCUS
No time to play, Braxus. Orders.

CRASSUS
Orders? Who's listening to orders today? Come on, Marcus! We've waited three years for this. Don't let orders get in your way.

MARCUS
Orders from the boss.

CRASSUS
Oh. General Marcellus?

MARCUS
So I'm told.

CRASSUS
Better get on with it then. Come on, partner, we've got some burning and looting
to do.

> (They both laugh, slap each other on the shoulders, and
> run away. LUCIUS opens the door and steps out. HELENA
> and CORNELIA follow him.)

MARCUS
Took you long enough. Let's go!

LUCIUS
The mistress Helena is ready. Eratosthenes, the son, is getting his father.

MARCUS
He's not ready? What's taking him so long?

LUCIUS
The master...he's finishing his work.

MARCUS
He's what!? What does he thinks going on here, a festival!? Doesn't he know his city
is being destroyed!?

LUCIUS
Festival. Destruction. It's all the same to Archimedes. His work is all that matters.

MARCUS
(pushing LUCIUS aside)
Get out of the way! I'll take care of this.

> (MARCUS enters the house and looks down at
> ARCHIMEDES.)

You there, are you the one they call Archimedes?

ERATOSTHENES
(to MARCUS)
Stand back.
(gently but urgently)
Papa, it's time to go.

ARCHIMEDES
(not even looking up)
Not just yet. I'm this close.

ERATOSTHENES
Papa, no! We must go now!

MARCUS
Come on, old man. Get up! Let's go!

ARCHIMEDES
Eh? Who are you? What business do you have in my house? Leave at once!

ERATOSTHENES
Papa!!!

MARCUS
Come on, old man. I haven't got all day!
(He steps onto the sand-tray.)

ARCHIMEDES
Here! Get off my board! You're standing on my drawing, you stupid oaf!

MARCUS
Get up, old man, or I'll give you something that'll make you get up!

ARCHIMEDES
Let go of me! What do you think…?

(MARCUS drags ARCHIMEDES out through the door and pushes him into the street.)

MARCUS
Just shut up and follow my orders.
(turning to ERATOSTHENES, who has followed them out)
You there, make him do as I…

(ARCHIMEDES strikes him with his compass.)

Ow! Why you nasty old vulture, hit me, will you? I'll show you what it means to strike a Roman soldier!

ERATOSTHENES
NO!!!

> *(MARCUS runs his sword through ARCHIMEDES who slumps to the ground. HELENA screams and clutches CORNELIA in horror. There is shocked silence, which is suddenly broken by an angry ERATOSTHENES. He rushes at MARCUS.)*

Why, you piece of Roman scum!

MARCUS
(struggling with, and pushing ERATOSTHENES away)
Get away from me, or you'll taste my sword, too!

> *(ERATOSTHENES rushes at MARCUS again, but MARCUS has his sword ready, and ERATOSTHENES is slain. HELENA utters a mournful sound and faints at CORNELIA's side. LUCIUS stares in pure hatred at the Roman).*

What are you staring at? You saw what they tried to do. I had my orders. What else was I supposed to do?

LUCIUS
You murdered them! You didn't need to...

MARCUS
I did what any Roman soldier would do! What are you sniveling about, anyway? They're Greeks. What does it matter to you? You're Roman, aren't you?

LUCIUS
(almost to himself)
Not any more.

MARCUS
Eh? Listen, you and I, we're in this together, right? We're both Romans. We stick up for each other.

LUCIUS
If you say so.

MARCUS
You're not going to say anything about this, are you? To the general, I mean?
(LUCIUS is silent)
Because...if you were planning on saying something I might have to...

> *(As he speaks, MARCUS begins to raise his sword*
> *threateningly. Suddenly LUCIUS bolts and exits.*
> *MARCUS is momentarily surprised.)*

Hey! Stop! Come back!

> *(He pauses to look at HELENA and CORNELIA, the other*
> *witnesses, uncertain as to what to do. Then he runs off-*
> *stage after LUCIUS.)*

SCENE 12

SETTING: (In front of ARCHIMEDES' house. MARCELLUS paces angrily, then
            confronts CLAUDIUS. LUCIUS, LIVIA, HELENA and CORNELIA stand
            dejectedly by)

MARCELLUS
I said he was not to be harmed! How could you let this happen?

CLAUDIUS
I gave your orders just as you gave them to me. The soldier...the soldier who killed
Archimedes told me he resisted departure. Archimedes refused to cooperate. And
then he hit the soldier.

MARCELLUS
(holding up the compass, then handing it to CLAUDIUS)
With a compass. A wooden compass!

CLAUDIUS
The soldier didn't tell me that.

MARCELLUS
I'm sure he didn't. He didn't tell you how he bullied his wife and murdered his son
either, did he?

CLAUDIUS
No. How do you know this?

MARCELLUS
(He gestures towards LUCIUS. LUCIUS looks up miserably.)
His servant told me.

CLAUDIUS
What will you have me do with the soldier?

MARCELLUS
He will receive the same treatment he gave that defenseless old man.
He is a traitor. Make him suffer.

CLAUDIUS
Aye, Sir.
(He is about to depart, then remembers something.)
Sir?

MARCELLUS
What is it?

CLAUDIUS
The soldiers found something in Archimedes' house. It looks valuable.
We thought you should see it.

MARCELLUS
(without enthusiasm)
Alright.

> *(CLAUDIUS picks up a large copper cylinder and copper
> sphere and hands them to MARCELLUS. MARCELLUS
> examines the objects with interest.)*

A cylinder and a sphere. And the sphere just barely fits inside the cylinder. Nice
craftsmanship. I wonder what it's for.

CLAUDIUS
Blessed if I know.

LIVIA
Master said with these objects he could go one better on his old friend from
Alexandria, the one who measured the distance around the earth.

MARCELLUS
How so?

LIVIA
Master said with this knowledge he could tell them the volume of the earth…
if anyone cared to know.

MARCELLUS
If anyone cared to know.

LUCIUS
Master said….

MARCELLUS
Yes?

LUCIUS
(he looks back to HELENA, who nods approvingly. MARCELLUS follows his glance.)
Master said he wanted the image of the sphere and cylinder engraved on his tomb.
He wanted to be remembered for it.

MARCELLUS
(a solemn pause)
He shall have his wish.

> *(MARCELLUS bows most respectfully to HELENA. As
> LUCIUS, LIVIAS, and MARCELLUS sing their personal
> eulogies to ARCHIMEDES, the full cast joins voices to
> conclude the song and play).*

LUCIUS AND LIVIA
    LONG AGO, SO LONG AGO, WHEN WE WERE BOTH SO YOUNG
    TO THIS ISLE OUR PARENTS FOUND THEIR WAY,
    SOLD AS SLAVES TO FOLK WHO SPOKE A VERY FOREIGN TONGUE,
    HARDLY KNOWING WHAT TO DO OR SAY.
    ARCHIMEDES TOOK THEM IN AS FAMILY,
    AS THEY LOOKED AWAY WITH EYES DOWNCAST;
    TREATED THEM WITH KINDNESS AND WITH DIGNITY,
    MAKING THEM FORGET THEIR BITTER PAST.

    SO WE GREW UP HAPPY IN A WARM AND LOVING HOME,
    NEVER KNOWING CRUELTY OR SHAME,

NEVER FEELING WE WERE CAPTIVE, LOST, OR ALL ALONE,
THOUGH WE MAY BE ROMANS BOTH IN NAME.
NOW YOU SAY WE'RE FREE FROM BONDAGE TO OUR FOE,
NOW WE CAN RETURN UNTO OUR KIN,
DON'T YOU SEE YOU'VE TAKEN EV'RYTHING WE OWN?
DON'T YOU SEE THE MISERY WE'RE IN?

MARCELLUS
I'VE BEEN A LOYAL ROMAN ALL MY LIFE,
DEDICATED TO THE DEEDS OF WAR;
NOT QUESTIONING THIS NECESSARY STRIFE,
ACCUSTOMED TO THE BLOODSHED AND THE GORE;
BUT TODAY I WONDER WHAT HAS BEEN THE COST
OF THE VICTORY WE SOUGHT SO LONG,
WEIGHED AGAINST THE NOBLE LIFE THAT HAS BEEN LOST,
CAN IT BE THAT ANYBODY WON?

ENTIRE CHORUS
LONG AGO, UPON THIS ISLAND IN THE SUN,
ARCHIMEDES DREW UPON THE SAND,
SEEKING ANSWERS TO THE QUESTIONS HE HAD SPUN,
QUESTIONS VERY FEW COULD UNDERSTAND.
FEW WERE THEY THAT HE COULD COUNT AMONG HIS FRIENDS,
FEW WERE THEY WHO RECOGNIZED HIS GRACE,
FEWER STILL WERE THOSE WHO UNDERSTOOD HIS ENDS,
FEW COULD TRAVEL TO HIS OTHER PLACE.
FEW STILL TRAVEL TO HIS OTHER PLACE, HIS OTHER PLACE.

THE END

MUSICAL SCORES

EUREKA!

OVERTURE

Lyrics by
JOHN TREVILLION

Music by
JEFFREY SPADE

© 2013

2

OVERTURE

83

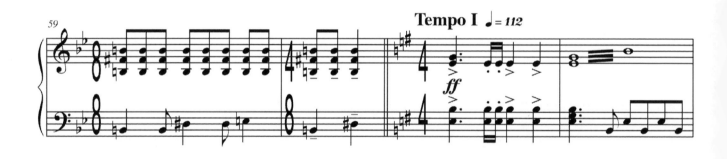

WE ARE ROMANS!

CUE: We are Romans!

Lyrics by
JOHN TREVILLION

Music by
JEFFREY SPADE

fight to save her ho - nor with e - v'ry-thing he's worth, He's loy - al to the ci - ty that will

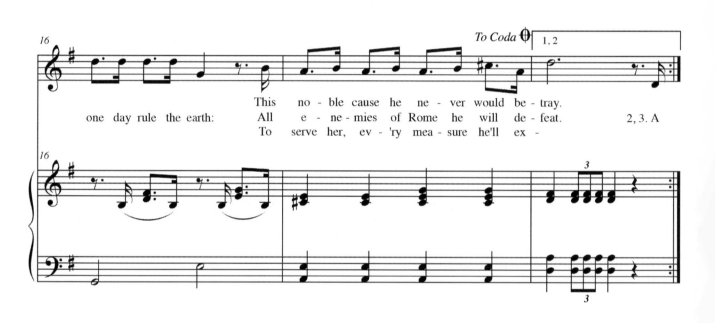

one day rule the earth:
This no - ble cause he ne - ver would be - tray.
All e - ne - mies of Rome he will de - feat.
To serve her, ev - 'ry mea - sure he'll ex -

2, 3. A

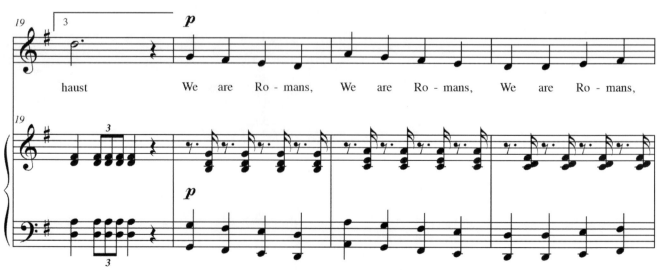

haust   We are Ro - mans, We are Ro - mans, We are Ro - mans,

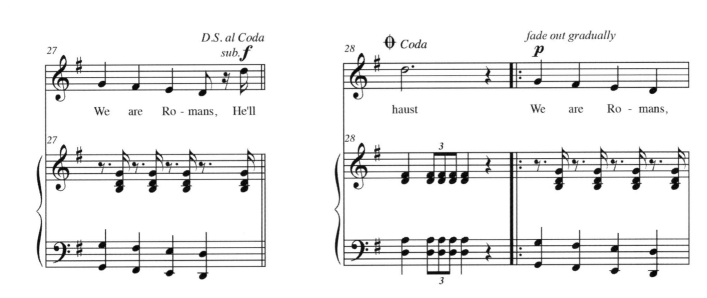

SCENE CHANGE 1

SCENE CHANGE 2

© 2013

SCENE CHANGE 3

CUE: *Go on.*

IN THAT OTHER PLACE

CUE: *No, not really.*

Lyrics by
JOHN TREVILLION

Music by
JEFFREY SPADE

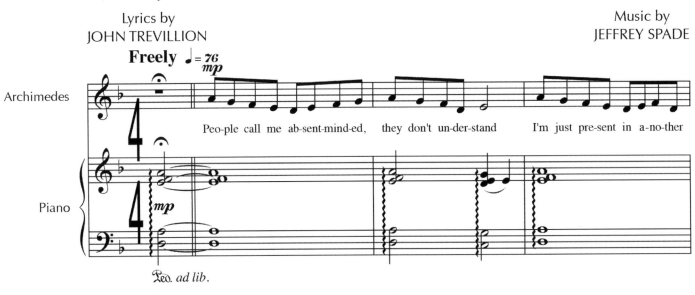

Peo-ple call me ab-sent-mind-ed, they don't un-der-stand I'm just pre-sent in a-no-ther

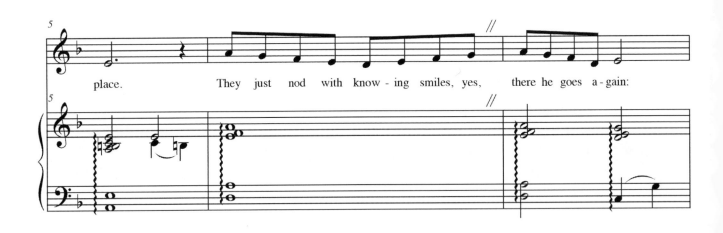

place. They just nod with know-ing smiles, yes, there he goes a-gain:

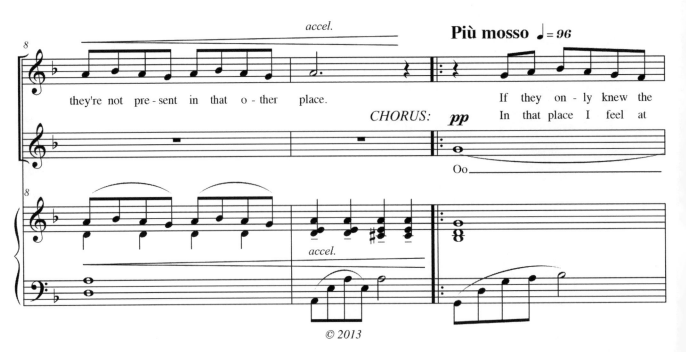

they're not pre-sent in that o-ther place.

CHORUS: *pp*

If they on-ly knew the
In that place I feel at

Oo

90

Tempo I

Helena

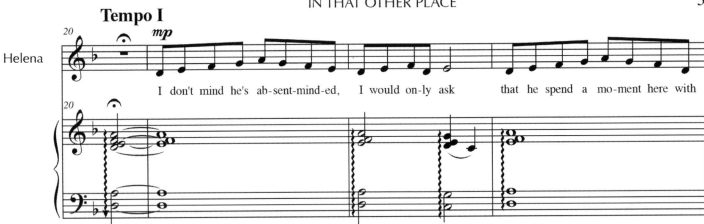

I don't mind he's ab-sent-mind-ed, I would on-ly ask that he spend a mo-ment here with

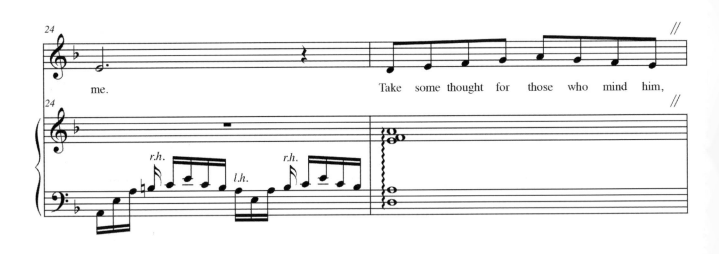

me. Take some thought for those who mind him,

look up from his task and al-low him-self to be with me.

Tempo I

Arch.

In the dis-tant land of E-gypt there's a place I know; I am not a stran-ger in that

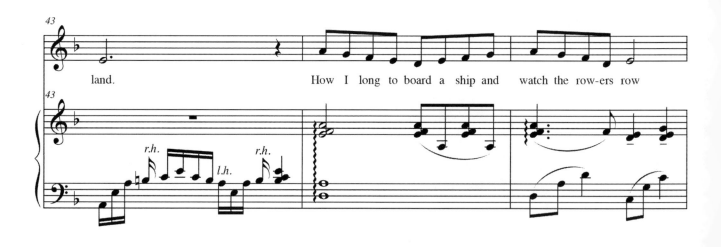

land. How I long to board a ship and watch the row-ers row

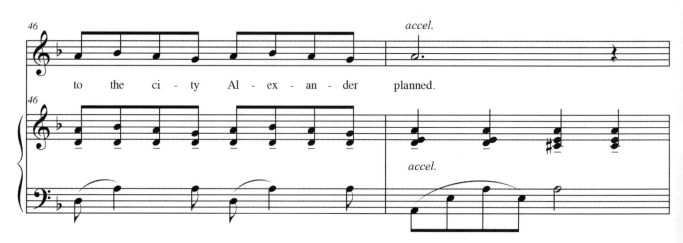

to the ci-ty Al-ex-an-der planned.

IN THAT OTHER PLACE

SCENE CHANGE 4

MECHANICAL ADVANTAGE

CUE: Explain.

Lyrics by
JOHN TREVILLION

Music by
JEFFREY SPADE

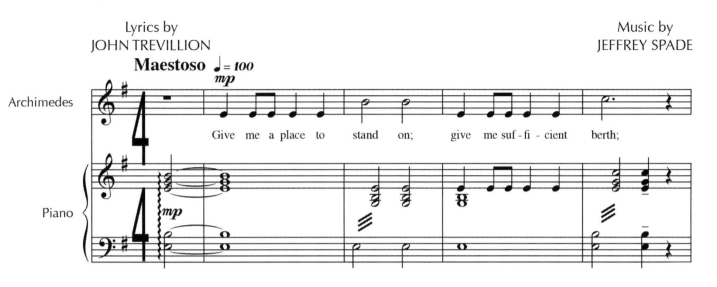

Give me a place to stand on; give me suf - fi - cient berth;

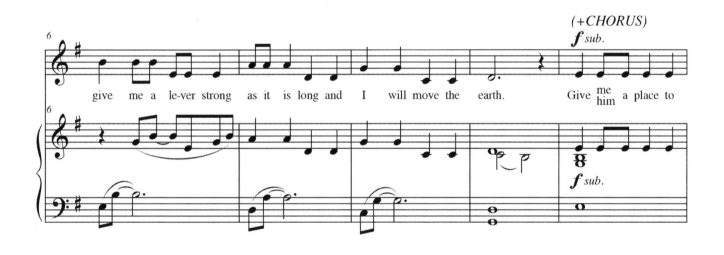

give me a le-ver strong as it is long and I will move the earth. Give me/him a place to

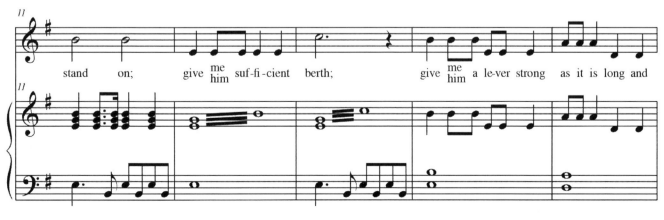

stand on; give me/him suf-fi-cient berth; give me/him a le-ver strong as it is long and

MECHANICAL ADVANTAGE

(-CHORUS)

he/I will move the earth. Give me a few round pul - leys; give me some rope un -

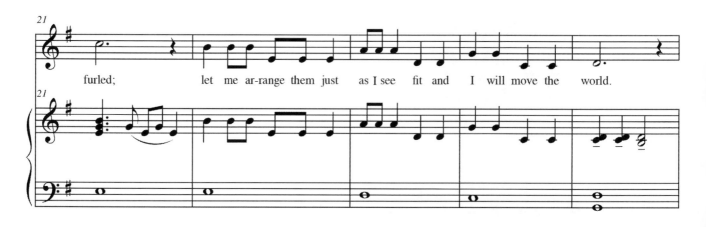

furled; let me ar-range them just as I see fit and I will move the world.

(+CHORUS)

Give me/him a few round pul - leys; give me/him some rope un - furled;

let me/him ar-range them just as I/he see(s) fit and I/he will move the world.

SCENE CHANGE 5

CUE: Archimedes must learn by himself where his
heart belongs, and I will give him all the time he needs.

EUREKA!

CUE: Master! Come back! I've got your clothes here!

Lyrics by
JOHN TREVILLION

Music by
JEFFREY SPADE

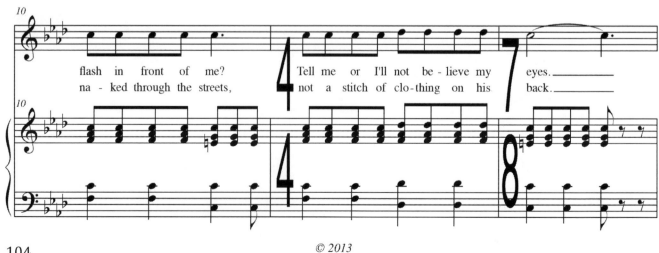

EUREKA!

SCENE CHANGE 6

© 2013

SCENE CHANGE 7

ISLAND OF THE SUN

CUE: *Let's make some music together.*

Lyrics by
JOHN TREVILLION

Music by
JEFFREY SPADE
& JOHN TREVILLION

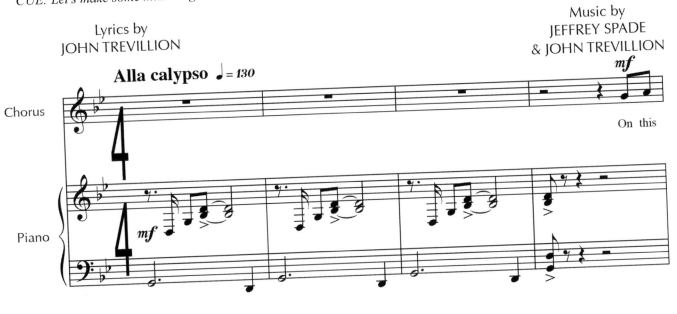

Chorus

Piano

On this

is - land of the sun, where Per - se - pho - ne as - cends to meet her mo - ther once a - gain; ___
is - land of the sun, where O - dys - se - us sought re - fuge on his wand - 'rings far from home, ___

and the face of Spring shines bright - ly as a -
it was here he met the Cy - clops who quite

phaes-tus stokes the fur-nace of his smi-thy un-der-ground;_____ and the
ci - ty mar-ried to the sea I call my ve-ry own;_____ where the

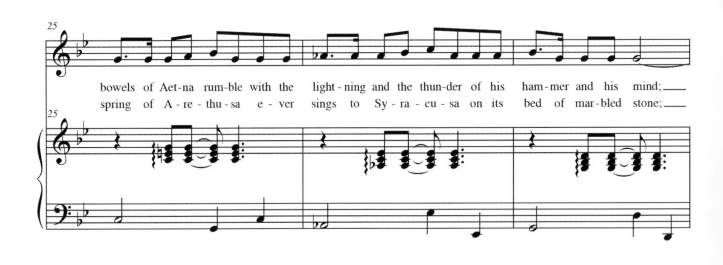

bowels of Aet-na rum-ble with the light-ning and the thun-der of his ham-mer and his mind;____
spring of A - re - thu - sa e - ver sings to Sy - ra - cu - sa on its bed of mar-bled stone;____

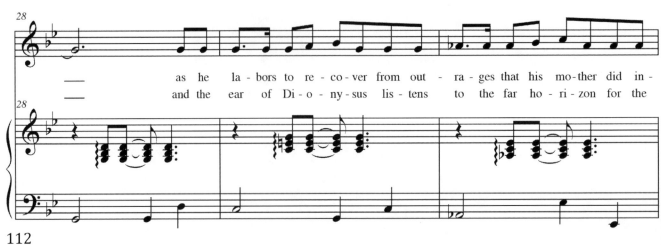

_____ as he la - bors to re - co - ver from out - ra - ges that his mo-ther did in -
_____ and the ear of Di - o - ny-sus lis - tens to the far ho - ri - zon for the

flict u-pon her son,_____ whose de - for-mi-ty she
sounds of dis - tant song,_____ on this

shunned, On this is - land of the sun. On this

is - land,_____ this is - land____ of the sun._____

SCENE CHANGE 8

© 2013

ENOUGH!

CUE: My Lord, you underestimate Hannibal...

Lyrics by
JOHN TREVILLION

Music by
JEFFREY SPADE

Hieron / Piano

E - nough! You tax my pa - tience and my mind; I warn you
you! You dis - sap - point my ve - ry soul; You have no

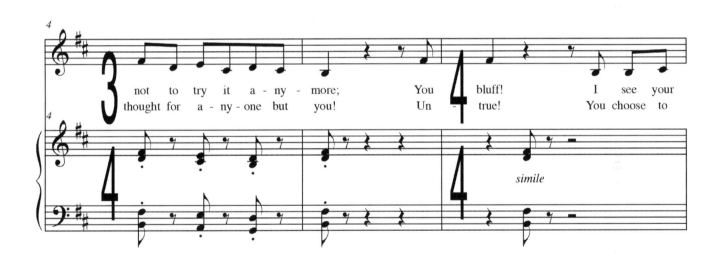

not to try it a - ny - more; You bluff! I see your
thought for a - ny - one but you! Un - true! You choose to

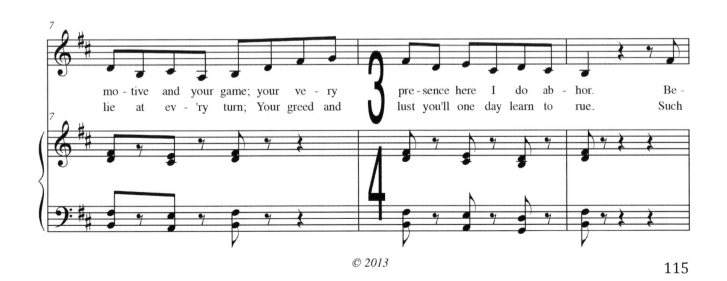

mo - tive and your game; your ve - ry pre - sence here I do ab - hor. Be -
lie at ev - 'ry turn; Your greed and lust you'll one day learn to rue. Such

2

ENOUGH!

e-ven now they laugh to hear me threa - ten them,

Tempo I

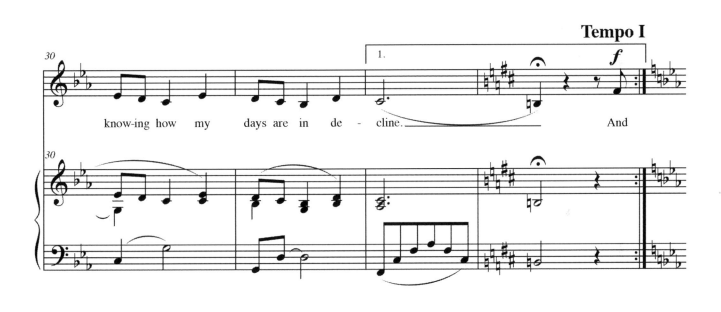

know-ing how my days are in de - cline. And

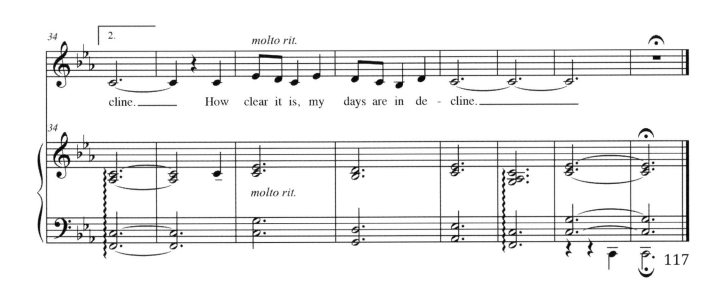

cline. How clear it is, my days are in de - cline.

HIERON'S FAREWELL

CUE: I would hear music to soothe the aching heart. And I would lie down.

© 2013

SCENE CHANGE 9

SCENE CHANGE 10

PIE (π) SONG

Lyrics by
JOHN TREVILLION

Music by
JOHN TREVILLION & JEFFREY SPADE

© 2013

EULOGY

CUE: He shall have his wish.

Lyrics by
JOHN TREVILLION

Music by
JEFFREY SPADE

Long a - go, so long a - go when we were both so young
So we grew up hap - py in a warm and lo - ving home,

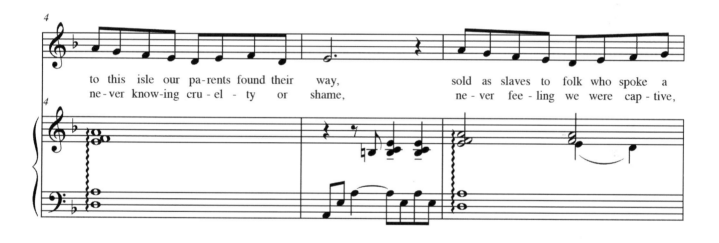

to this isle our pa - rents found their way, sold as slaves to folk who spoke a
ne - ver know - ing cru - el - ty or shame, ne - ver fee - ling we were cap - tive,

ve - ry fo - reign tongue, hard - ly know - ing what to do or say.
lost, or all a - lone, though we may be Ro - mans both in name.

gainst the no-ble life that has been lost, can it be that a-ny-bo-dy won?

Tempo II

COMPANY:

Long a - go, u-pon this is - land in ____ the sun, Ar - chi - me - des drew u -
Few were they that he could count a - mong ____ his friends, few were they who re - cog-

pon the sand, ____ see-king an - swers to the ques - tions he ____ had spun,
nized his grace, ____ few - er still were those who un - der - stood ____ his ends,

ques-tions ve - ry few could un - der - stand.
few could tra - vel to his o - ther ____

place.

Few still tra - vel to his o - ther place, his o - ther

place.

simile

ff

BOWS

END OF SHOW

© 2013

Made in the USA
Columbia, SC
24 November 2024